ONE STORY HOMES

Under 2,000 Sq. Ft. • Traditional & Contemporary Styles

HOME PLANNERS, INC.

Contents

Published by Home Planners, Inc., 23761 Research Drive, Farmington Hills, Michigan 48024.
All designs and illustrative material Copyright © MCMLXXXVI by Home Planners, Inc. All
rights reserved. Reproduction in any manner or form not permitted. Printed in the United
States of America. International Standard Book Number (ISBN): 0-918894-52-2.

Distributed by HPBooks, Inc.

Index to Designs

On the Cover: Cover design can be found on page 28.

How To Read Floor Plans and Blueprints

Selecting the most suitable house plan for your family is a matter of matching your needs, tastes, and life-style against the many designs we offer. When you study the floor plans in this issue, and the blueprints that you may subsequently order, remember that they are simply a two-dimensional representation of what will eventually be a three-dimensional reality.

Floor plans are easy to read. Rooms are clearly labeled, with dimensions given in feet and inches. Most symbols are logical and self-explanatory: The location of bathroom fixtures, planters, fireplaces, tile floors, cabinets and counters, sinks, appliances, closets, sloped or beamed ceilings will be obvious.

A blueprint, although much more detailed, is also easy to read; all it demands is concentration. The blueprints that we offer come in many large sheets, each one of which contains a different kind of information. One sheet contains foundation and excavation drawings, another has a precise plot plan. An elevations sheet deals with the exterior walls of the house; section drawings show precise dimensions, fittings, doors, windows, and roof structures. Our detailed floor plans give the construction information needed by your contractor. And each set of blueprints contains a lengthy materials list with size and quantities of all necessary components. Using this list, a contractor and suppliers can make a start at calculating costs for you.

When you first study a floor plan or blueprint, imagine that you are walking through the house. By mentally visualizing each room in three dimensions, you can transform the technical data and symbols into something more real.

Start at the front door. It's preferable to have a foyer or entrance hall in which to receive guests. A closet here is desirable; a powder room is a plus.

Look for good traffic circulation as you study the floor plan. You should not have to pass all the way through one main room to reach another. From the entrance area you should have direct access to the three principal areas of a house—the living, work, and sleeping zones. For example, a foyer might provide separate entrances to the living room, kitchen, patio, and a hallway or staircase leading to the bedrooms.

Study the layout of each zone. Most people expect the living room to be protected from cross traffic. The kitchen, on the other hand, should connect with the dining room—and perhaps also the utility room, basement, garage, patio or deck, or a secondary entrance. A homemaker whose workday centers in the kitchen may have special requirements: a window that faces the backyard; a clear view of the family room where children play; a garage or driveway entrance that

allows for a short trip with groceries; laundry facilities close at hand. Check for efficient placement of kitchen cabinets, counters, and appliances. Is there enough room in the kitchen for additional appliances, for eating in? Is there a dining nook?

Perhaps this part of the house contains a family room or a den/bedroom/office. It's advantageous to have a bathroom or powder room in this section.

As you study the plan, you may encounter a staircase, indicated by a group of parallel lines, the number of lines equaling the number of steps. Arrows labeled "up" mean that the staircase leads to a higher level, and those pointing down mean it leads to a lower one. Staircases in a split-level will have both up and down arrows on one staircase because two levels are depicted in one drawing and an extra level in another.

Notice the location of the stairways. Is too much floor space lost to them? Will you find yourself making too many trips?

Study the sleeping quarters. Are the bedrooms situated as you like? You may want the master bedroom near the kids, or you may want it as far away as possible. Is there at least one closet per person in each bedroom or a double one for a couple? Bathrooms should be convenient to each bedroom—if not adjoining, then with hallway access and on the same floor.

Once you are familiar with the relative positions of the rooms, look for such structural details as:

• Sufficient uninterrupted wall space for furniture arrangement.

• Adequate room dimensions.

• Potential heating or cooling problems—i.e., a room over a garage or next to the laundry.

• Window and door placement for good ventilation and natural light.

• Location of doorways—avoid having a basement staircase or a bathroom in view of the dining room.

• Adequate auxiliary space—closets, storage, bathrooms, countertops.

• Separation of activity areas. (Will noise from the recreation room disturb sleeping children or a parent at work?)

As you complete your mental walk through the house, bear in mind your family's long-range needs. A good house plan will allow for some adjustments now and additions in the future.

Each member of your family may find the listing of his, or her, favorite features a most helpful exercise. Why not try it?

How To Choose a Contractor

A contractor is part craftsman, part businessman, and part magician. As the person who will transform your dreams and drawings into a finished house, he will be responsible for the final cost of the structure, for the quality of the workmanship, and for the solving of all problems that occur quite naturally in the course of construction. Choose him as carefully as you would a business partner, because for the next several months that will be his role in your life.

As soon as you have a building site and house plans, start looking for a contractor, even if you do not plan to break ground for several months. Finding one suitable to build your house can take time, and once you have found him, you will have to be worked into his schedule. Those who are good are in demand and, where the season is short, they are often scheduling work up to a year in advance.

There are two types of residential contractors: the construction company and the carpenter-builder, often called a general contractor. Each of these has its advantages and disadvantages.

The carpenter-builder works directly on the job as the field foreman. Because his background is that of a craftsman, his workmanship is probably good—but his paperwork may be slow or sloppy. His overhead—which you pay for—is less than that of a large construction company. However, if the job drags on for any reason, his interest may flag because your project is overlapping his next job and eroding his profits.

Construction companies handle several projects concurrently. They have an office staff to keep the paperwork moving and an army of subcontractors they know they can count on. Though you can be confident that they will meet deadlines, they may sacrifice workmanship in order to do so. Because they emphasize efficiency, they are less personal to work with than a general contractor. Many will not work with an individual unless he is represented by an architect. The company and the architect speak the same language; it requires far more time to deal directly with a homeowner.

To find a reliable contractor, start by asking friends who have built homes for recommendations. Check with local lumber yards and building supply outlets for names of possible candidates.

Once you have several names in hand, ask the Chamber of Commerce, Better Business Bureau, or local department of consumer affairs for any information they might have on each of them. Keep in mind that these watchdog organizations can give only the number of complaints filed; they cannot tell you what percent of those claims were valid. Remember, too, that a large-volume operation is logically going to have more complaints against it than will an independent contractor.

Set up an interview with each of the potential candidates. Find out what his specialty is—custom houses, development houses, remodeling, or office buildings. Ask each to take you into—not just to the site of—houses he has built. Ask to see projects that are complete as well as work in progress, emphasizing that you are interested in projects comparable to yours. A $300,000 dentist's office will give you little insight into a contractor's craftsmanship.

Ask each contractor for bank references from both his commercial bank and any other lender he has worked with. If he is in good financial standing, he should have no qualms about giving you this information. Also ask if he offers a warranty on his work. Most will give you a one-year warranty on the structure; some offer as much as a ten-year warranty.

Ask for references, even though no contractor will give you the name of a dissatisfied customer. While previous clients may be pleased with a contractor's work overall, they may, for example, have had to wait three months after they moved in before they had any closet doors. Ask about his follow-through. Did he clean up the building site, or did the owner have to dispose of the refuse? Ask about his business organization. Did the paperwork go smoothly, or was there a delay in hooking up the sewer because he forgot to apply for a permit?

Talk to each of the candidates about fees. Most work on a "cost plus" basis; that is, the basic cost of the project—materials, subcontractors' services, wages of those working directly on the project, but not office help—plus his fee. Some have a fixed fee; others work on a percentage of the basic cost. A fixed fee is usually better for you if you can get one. If a contractor works on a percentage, ask for a cost breakdown of his best estimate and keep very careful track as the work progresses. A crafty contractor can always use a cost overrun to his advantage when working on a percentage.

Do not be overly suspicious of a contractor who won't work on a fixed fee. One who is very good and in great demand may not be willing to do so. He may also refuse to submit a competitive bid.

If the top two or three candidates are willing to submit competitive bids, give each a copy of the plans and your specifications for materials. If they are not each working from the same guidelines, the competitive bids will be of little value. Give each the same deadline for turning in a bid; two or three weeks is a reasonable period of time. If you are willing to go with the lowest bid, make an appointment with all of them and open the envelopes in front of them.

If one bid is remarkably low, the contractor may have made an honest error in his estimate. Do not try to hold him to it if he wants to withdraw his bid. Forcing him to build at too low a price could be disastrous for both you and him.

Though the above method sounds very fair and orderly, it is not always the best approach, especially if you are inexperienced. You may want to review the bids with your architect, if you have one, or with your lender to discuss which to accept. They may not recommend the lowest. A low bid does not necessarily mean that you will get quality with economy.

If the bids are relatively close, the most important consideration may not be money at all. How easily you can talk with a contractor and whether or not he inspires confidence are very important considerations. Any sign of a personality conflict between you and a contractor should be weighed when making a decision.

Once you have financing, you can sign a contract with the builder. Most have their own contract forms, but it is advisable to have a lawyer draw one up or, at the very least, review the standard contract. This usually costs a small flat fee.

A good contract should include the following:
• Plans and sketches of the work to be done, subject to your approval.
• A list of materials, including quantity, brand names, style or serial numbers. (Do not permit any "or equal" clause that will allow the contractor to make substitutions.)
• The terms—who (you or the lender) pays whom and when.
• A production schedule.
• The contractor's certification of insurance for workmen's compensation, damage, and liability.
• A rider stating that all changes, whether or not they increase the cost, must be submitted and approved in writing.

Of course, this list represents the least a contract should include. Once you have signed it, your plans are on the way to becoming a home.

A frequently asked question is: "Should I become my own general contractor?" Unless you have knowledge of construction, material purchasing, and experience supervising subcontractors, we do not recommend this route.

How To Shop For Mortgage Money

Most people who are in the market for a new home spend months searching for the right house plan and building site. Ironically, these same people often invest very little time shopping for the money to finance their new home, though the majority will have to live with the terms of their mortgage for as long as they live in the house.

The fact is that all banks are not alike, nor are the loans that they offer—and banks are not the only financial institutions that lend money for housing. The amount of down payment, interest rate, and period of the mortgage are all, to some extent, negotiable.

• Lending practices vary from one city and state to another. If you are a first-time builder or are new to an area, it is wise to hire a real estate (not divorce or general practice) attorney to help you unravel the maze of your specific area's laws, ordinances, and customs.

• Before talking with lenders, write down all your questions. Take notes during the conversation so you can make accurate comparisons.

• Do not be intimidated by financial officers. Keep in mind that you *are not begging for money*, you are buying it. Do not hesitate to reveal what other institutions are offering; they may be challenged to meet or better the terms.

• Use whatever clout you have. If you or your family have been banking with the same firm for years, let them know that they could lose your business if you can get a better deal elsewhere.

• Know your credit rights. The law prohibits lenders from considering only the husband's income when determining eligibility, a practice that previously kept many people out of the housing market. If you are turned down for a loan, you have a right to see a summary of the credit report and change any errors in it.

A GUIDE TO LENDERS

Where can you turn for home financing? Here is a list of sources for you to approach:

Savings and loan associations are the best place to start because they write well over half the mortgages in the United States on dwellings that house from one to four families. They generally offer favorable interest rates, require lower down payments, and allow more time to pay off loans than do other banks.

Savings banks, sometimes called mutual savings banks, are your next best bet. Like savings and loan associations, much of their business is concentrated in home mortgages.

Commercial banks write mortgages as a sideline, and when money is tight many will not write mortgages at all. They do hold about 15 percent of the mortgages in the country, however, and when the market is right, they can be very competitive.

Mortgage banking companies use the money of private investors to write home loans. They do a brisk business in government-backed loans, which other banks are reluctant to handle because of the time and paperwork required.

Some credit unions are now allowed to grant mortgages. A few insurance companies, pension funds, unions, and fraternal organizations also offer mortgage money to their membership, often at terms more favorable than those available in the commercial marketplace.

A GUIDE TO MORTGAGES

The types of mortgages available are far more various than most potential home buyers realize.

Traditional Loans

Conventional home loans have a fixed interest rate and fixed monthly payments. About 80 percent of the mortgage money in the United States is lent in this manner. Made by private lending institutions, these fixed rate loans are available to anyone whom the bank officials consider a good credit risk. The interest rate depends on the prevailing market for money and is slightly negotiable if you are willing to put down a large down payment. Most down payments range from 15 to 33 percent.

You can borrow as much money as the lender believes you can afford to pay off over the negotiated period of time—usually 20 to 30 years. However, a 15 year mortgage can save you considerably and enable you to own your home in half the time. For example, a 30 year, $60,800 mortgage at 12% interest will have a monthly payment of $625.40 per month vs $729.72 per month for a 15 year loan at the same interest rate. At the end of 30 years you have paid $164,344 in interest vs $70,550 for the 15 year. Remember - this is only $104.32 more per month. Along with saving with a 15 year mortgage, additional savings

can be realized with a biweekly payment plan. So be sure to consult your borrowing institution for all of your options.

The FHA does not write loans; it insures them against default in order to encourage lenders to write loans for first-time buyers and people with limited incomes. The terms of these loans make them very attractive, and you may be allowed to take as long as 25 to 30 years to pay it off.

The down payment also is substantially lower with an FHA-backed loan. At present it is set at 3 percent of the first $25,000 and 5 percent of the remainder, up to the $75,300 limit. This means that a loan on a $75,300 house would require a $750 down payment on the first $25,000 plus $2,515 on the remainder, for a total down payment of $3,265. In contrast, the down payment for the same house financed with a conventional loan could run as high as $20,000.

Anyone may apply for an FHA-insured loan, but both the borrower and the house must qualify.

The VA guarantees loans for eligible veterans, and the husbands and wives of those who died while in the service or from a service-related disability. The VA guarantees up to 60 percent of the loan or $27,500, whichever is less. Like the FHA, the VA determines the appraised value of the house, though with a VA loan, you can borrow any amount up to the appraised value.

The Farmers Home Administration offers the only loans made directly by the government. Families with limited incomes in rural areas can qualify if the house is in a community of less than 10,000 people and is outside of a large metropolitan area; if their income is less than $18,000; and if they can prove that they do not qualify for a conventional loan.

For more information, write Farmers Home Administration, Department of Agriculture, Washington, D.C. 20250, or your local office.

New loan instruments

If you think that the escalating cost of housing has squeezed you out of the market, take a look at the following new types of mortgages.

The graduated payment mortgage features a monthly obligation that gradually increases over a negotiated period of time—usually five to ten years. Though the payments begin lower, they stabilize at a higher monthly rate than a standard fixed rate mortgage. Little or no equity is built in the first years, a disadvantage if you decide to sell early in the mortgage period.

These loans are aimed at young people who can anticipate income increases that will enable them to meet the escalating payments. The size of the down payment is about the same or slightly higher than for a conventional loan, but you can qualify with a lower income. As of last year, savings and loan associations can write these loans, and the FHA now insures five different types.

The flexible loan insurance program (FLIP) requires that part of the down payment, which is about the same as a conventional loan, be placed in a pledged savings account. During the first five years of the mortgage, funds are drawn from this account to supplement the lower monthly payments.

The deferred interest mortgage, another graduated program, allows you to pay a lower rate of interest during the first few years and a higher rate in the later years of the mortgage. If the house is sold, the borrower must pay back all the interest, often with a prepayment penalty. Both the FLIP and deferred interest loans are very new and not yet widely available.

The variable rate mortgage is most widely available in California, but its popularity is growing. This instrument features a fluctuating interest rate that is linked to an economic indicator—usually the lender's cost of obtaining funds for lending. To protect the consumer against a sudden and disastrous increase, regulations limit the amount that the interest rate can increase over a given period of time.

To make these loans attractive, lenders offer them without prepayment penalties and with "assumption" clauses that allow another buyer to assume your mortgage should you sell.

Flexible payment mortgages allow young people who can anticipate rising incomes to enter the housing market sooner. They pay only the interest during the first few years; then the mortgage is amortized and the payments go up. This is a valuable option only for those people who intend to keep their home for several years because no equity is built in the lower payment period.

The reverse annuity mortgage is targeted for older people who have fixed incomes. This new loan allows those who qualify to tap into the equity on their houses. The lender pays them each month and collects the loan when the house is sold or the owner dies.

TRADITIONAL DESIGNS

1200-1599 Sq. Ft. . . . *as*

featured in the following pages, capture the warmth and charm of an early period in our history. Here we see appealing examples of the one-story house reflecting the beauty that results from effective and prudent use of early American design features. These include, double-hung, muntined windows, panelled doors with side lights, shutters, cupolas, flower boxes, carriage lamps, wood siding with corner boards, covered front entrances, etc. And above all, pleasing proportion is a prime requisite for achieving that delightful exterior appeal that assures a lasting value for, perhaps, life's biggest single investment. Here are houses for the modest budget.

Design 32707 1,267 Sq. Ft.; 27,125 Cu. Ft.

● Here is a charming Early American adaptation that will serve as a picturesque and practical retirement home. Also, it will serve admirably those with a small family in search of an efficient, economically built home. The living area, highlighted by the raised hearth fireplace, is spacious. The kitchen features eating space and easy access to the garage and basement. The dining room is adjacent to the kitchen and views the rear yard. Then, there is the basement for recreation and hobby pursuits. The bedroom wing offers three bedrooms and two full baths. Don't miss the sliding doors to the terrace from the living room and the master bedroom. Storage units are plentiful including a pantry cabinet in the eating area of the kitchen. This plan will be efficient and livable.

Design 31025 1,426 Sq. Ft.; 28,277 Cu. Ft.

● A real charmer. At the front of the house, parents have a private master suite with a full bath and generous closet space. Opposite the master bedroom is a secluded living room, without any through-traffic, and a center fireplace that provides a focus of interest for arranging furniture. Recreational facilities may be developed in the full basement. This area also lends itself to developing additional storage.

● This traditional one-story home with its attached two-car garage virtually overflows with livability. There is not a foot of wasted space incorporated in this plan. Seldom is such good use made of a nominal amount of space. This home can be called upon to function as either a three or a four bedroom home. If the former, then the extra room may be utilized as a family room or study. There are two eating areas.

Design 33204 1,250 Sq. Ft.; 24,475 Cu. Ft.

Design 31024 1,252 Sq. Ft.; 23,925 Cu. Ft.

● "Charming", is but one of the many words that could be chosen to describe this traditional home. While essentially a frame house, the front exterior features natural quarried stone. Below the overhanging roof, the windows and door treatment is most pleasing. The board fence with its lamp post completes a delightful picture. Highlighting the interior is the living room with its raised hearth fireplace.

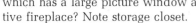

● With the kitchen in this strategic location, the homemaker does not have to go through half of the house in order to get to the front door. The second bath with its stall shower is convenient to the third bedroom, the family area and the outdoor terrace. The main bath has a delightful built-in vanity. And how about the living room which has a large picture window and an attractive fireplace? Note storage closet.

Design 31197 1,232 Sq. Ft.; 24,123 Cu. Ft.

9

Design 31173
1,500 Sq. Ft.; 18,230 Cu. Ft.

● A picturesque, L-shaped traditional one-story with an attractive, covered porch. This floor plan is wonderfully zoned. All the major areas are but a few steps from the front entry hall. The living room with its bay window enables one to have a delightful view of the rear yard. It will lend itself to fine furniture arrangements and be free of cross-room traffic, too. Three bedrooms in the sleeping area plus a full bath. The homemaker will love the efficient kitchen as well as the separate laundry area. The extra washroom, through the laundry, is handy from the outdoors. The favorite spot will be the large family room. This multi-purpose area functions well with the kitchen. Built-in china cabinets are located in the two front corners of this area. Certainly a delightful feature. Two storage areas are in the garage. Note that the garage can be built to accommodate either one or two cars.

Design 31193
1,396 Sq. Ft.; 17,213 Cu. Ft.

● This L-shaped, one-story with its attached two-car garage incorporates many of the time-tested features of older New England. The attractive cut-up windows, the shutters, the panelled door, the fence and the wood siding contribute to the charm of the exterior. The floor plan is outstanding by virtue of such proven features as the separate dining room, the family-kitchen, the quiet living room with its bay window and the privacy of the bedroom area. The U-shaped work center will be easy to work in.

Design 31327
1,392 Sq. Ft.; 18,480 Cu. Ft.

● A design to overcome the restrictions of a relatively narrow building site. This home has one of the best one-story plans you'll ever see. Its four bedrooms and two baths form what amounts to a separate wing. The fourth bedroom is located next to the living room so it may serve as a study, if needed. The traffic plan pivoting in the front entry, is excellent. And the kitchen is in just the right place - next to the dining and family rooms, close to the front and side doors and near the laundry. Another fine quality of the kitchen is its snack bar pass-thru to the family room. Formal living will take place in the rear living/dining room. This area can open up to the rear terrace by two sets of sliding glass doors (another set is in the family room). An optional basement plan is included with the purchase of this design.

OPTIONAL BASEMENT PLAN

Design 31316
1,488 Sq. Ft.; 29,034 Cu. Ft.

● As picturesque as they come. Within 1,488 square feet, there are the fine sleeping facilities, two full baths, family room, a formal dining area, a big living room, an excellent kitchen and plenty of closets. Other noteworthy features include the fireplace, sliding glass doors to the rear terrace, a fine basement, a pass-thru to family room from kitchen, an attached garage and an appealing front porch.

OPTIONAL
NON - BASEMENT

Design 31939
1,387 Sq. Ft.; 28,000 Cu. Ft.

● A finely proportioned house with more than its full share of charm. The brick veneer exterior contrasts pleasingly with the narrow horizontal siding of the oversized attached two-car garage. Perhaps the focal point of the exterior is the recessed front entrance with its double Colonial styled doors. The secondary service entrance through the garage to the kitchen area is a handy feature. Study the plan. It features three bedrooms, two full baths, living room with fireplace, front kitchen with an eating area, formal dining room, plenty of storage potential plus a basement for additional storage or perhaps to be developed as a recreational area.

Design 31190
1,232 Sq. Ft.; 15,301 Cu. Ft.

● Build this L-shaped house on your lot with the garage door facing the street, or with the front entry door facing the street. Whichever orientation you choose, and you should take into consideration lot restriction and any particular view you might want to enjoy from the living areas, you will find the floor plan a very fine one. The center entrance hall features twin coat closets, a slate floor and an attractive six foot high room divider. This built-in unit has a planter on top with storage space below which is accessible from the living room.

Design 31944
1,474 Sq. Ft.; 16,626 Cu. Ft.

● Imagine, four bedrooms and two full baths in a home under 1,500 square feet. As if this wasn't enough to make this a home of distinction, there is an abundance of livability in the other half of the floor plan. Here, there is an excellent living room which looks out upon the rear terrace, a large family dining area and an efficient U-shaped kitchen. It will be difficult to find a better investment.

Design 31189
1,240 Sq. Ft.; 14,981 Cu. Ft.

● When you obtain the blueprints for this picturesque frame home you will receive details for both basement and non-basement construction. Whatever your choice of construction your family will love the basic livablility provided by the arrangement of the three bedrooms, two full baths, the formal living room, the family-dining room and the efficient U-shaped kitchen. The single car garage may be readily adapted to accommodate two cars. Note the three garage storage closets.

Design 31147
1,264 Sq. Ft.; 24,016 Cu. Ft.

● "Who could ask for anything more" is an appropriate theme for this house. It is easy on the budget with only 1,264 square feet, but it includes big-house features, such as four bedrooms, one-and-one-half baths, a fireplace, a family room and an over-sized garage, plus the convenience of more closets than the normal family would require. Don't miss the built-in chest, china cupboard and the kitchen cooking equipment.

Design 31074
1,356 Sq. Ft.; 25,431 Cu. Ft.

● There is much to consider when deciding upon the selection of this house as your new home. First of all, the exterior leaves nothing to be desired. It has exceptional eye appeal and will surely retain its charm for generations to come. The projecting bedroom wing, the attached two-car garage and the large covered front porch are major features which help set the character of the exterior. Then, the floor plan with its L-shaped zoning could hardly be improved upon.

Design 31075
1,232 Sq. Ft.; 24,123 Cu. Ft.

● This picturesque traditional one-story home has much to offer the young family. Because of its rectangular shape and its predominantly frame exterior, construction costs will be economical. Passing through the front entrance, visitors will be surprised to find so much livability in only 1,232 square feet. Consider these features: spacious formal living and dining area; two full baths; efficient kitchen; and large, rear family room. In addition there is the full basement for further recreational facilities and bulk storage. The attached garage is extra long to accommodate the storage of garden equipment, lawn furniture, bicycles, etc.

Design 31366
1,280 Sq. Ft.; 14,848 Cu. Ft.

● The extension of the main roof, along with the use of ornamental iron, vertical siding and glass side lites flanking the paneled door, all contribute to a delightful and inviting front entrance to this L-shaped design. There is much to recommend this design—from the attached two-car garage to the walk-in closet of the master bedroom. Don't overlook the compartmented master bath with its stall shower and powder room; the built-in china cabinet with an attractive planter above or the two closets right in the center of the house.

Design 31191
1,232 Sq. Ft.; 15,400 Cu. Ft.

● A careful study of the floor plan for this cozy appearing traditional home reveals a fine combination of features which add tremendously to convenient living. For instance, observe the wardrobe and storage facilities of the bedroom area. A built-in chest in the one bedroom and also one in the family room. Then, notice the economical plumbing of the two full back-to-back baths. Postively a great money saving feature for today and in the future. Further, don't overlook the location of the washer and dryer which have cupboards above the units themselves. Observe storage facilities. Optional two-car garage is available if necessary.

MASTER BED RM. 12⁸ x 10⁸

BATH

STUDY-DINING RM. 10⁴ x 10⁸

KIT. 11⁸ x 10⁸

FAMILY RM. 20⁰ x 11⁶

BATH LIN.

PANTRY REF'G

AIR COND.

CL.

BED RM. 10⁰ x 12⁴

BED RM. 10⁰ x 9⁰

ENTRY

LIVING RM. 16⁰ x 12⁴

OPTIONAL BASEMENT STAIRS

CURB

WINDOW SEAT

GARAGE 19⁸ x 23⁴

TERRACE

66'-10"

24'-0"

36'-10"

12'-0"

FENCE

● Brick veneer, a projecting two-car garage with a gabled end, wood shutters, attractive window treatment, paneled front door and a wood fence with lamp post are among the features that make the exterior of this traditional house so charming. The formal living room with all that blank wall space for effective furniture placement, is just the right size for quiet conversation. The family room will be the hub of the informal activities with a snack bar and pass-thru to the kitchen. Adjacent to the kitchen is a room which may function as a study, sewing room, TV room or formal dining room. Note the two full baths and stall shower.

Design 31367
1,432 Sq. Ft.; 16,611 Cu. Ft.

MASTER BED RM. 13⁰ x 11⁶

W.R.

FAMILY-DINING 12⁶ x 11⁶

KIT. 12⁰ x 11⁶

GARAGE 15⁸ x 23⁴

BATH

OVEN RANGE

CHINA

BED RM. 9⁸ x 9⁴

LIN.

STUDY-B.R. 10⁰ x 8⁰

CEILING DROP

ENTRY

LIVING RM. 19⁸ x 11⁶

STORAGE

BED RM. 13⁰ x 11⁸

CHEST

TERRACE

60'-10"

44'-5"

16'-5"

24'-0"

36'-10"

● A small house which includes a full measure of big house living features. The master bedroom has its extra washroom. In addition to the two bedrooms for the children, there is a study, or fourth bedroom. (This extra room offers the option to serve as a sewing, TV, music or even a guest room.) The living room is well situated and will not be bothered by cross-room traffic. The kitchen functions conveniently with the family-dining area. The stairs to the basement are just inside the entrance from the attached garage.

Design 31802
1,315 Sq. Ft.; 24,790 Cu. Ft.

Design 31094
1,484 Sq. Ft.; 29,057 Cu. Ft.

● Picturesque and practical are two words to aptly describe the merits of this fine L-shaped traditional home. The delightful proportion and the appealing details help create the charming image. The floor plan is a particularly well-planned one. In less than 1,500 square feet there are three bedrooms, 2½ baths, a family room, a 25 foot formal living and dining area, a strategically located kitchen, a first floor laundry and a basement. Other noteworthy features include the two fireplaces, the wood box, sliding glass doors to side terrace and excellent storage facilities throughout.

Design 31034
1,440 Sq. Ft.; 16,084 Cu. Ft.

● The curved drive approach to the projected garage of this delightfully traditional frame home helps complete an impressive picture. The salt box type roof of the garage, the cupola, the window treatment and the covered porch with its wood railing, make their vital contributions to the charm of the exterior. The two major living areas-the living and family rooms-look out upon, and function with, their own outdoor living terraces. Both of these indoor/outdoor areas enjoy privacy.

Design 33211
1,344 Sq. Ft.; 26,423 Cu. Ft.

● This is a captivating version of the three bedroom, two-bath L-shaped home. Notice that spacious living-dining area with the many windows to the side plus a view of the rear terrace from the dining room. The living room also has a fireplace for added appeal. The breakfast room also will enjoy the rear terrace and includes such features as a pantry, china cabinet and storage closet. The kitchen is an efficient work center with nearby adjacent basement stairs. The basement could be developed into an informal recreation area.

Design 31188
1,326 Sq. Ft.; 16,469 Cu. Ft.

● This charming, traditionally styled, L-shaped home can be built most economically. Constructed on a concrete slab, the house itself forms a perfect rectangle, thus assuring the most efficient use of materials. The center entrance routes traffic to the various areas of this plan most conveniently. Compact, yet spacious. The three bedrooms are sizable and enjoy their privacy. The entire breadth of the rear experiences the delightful feeling of openness.

Design 32122 *1,248 Sq. Ft.; 14,560 Cu. Ft.*

● An ideal home for a family of modest size with a modest budget. This charming frame house can be built most economically. The main portion of the

OPTIONAL BASEMENT PLAN

house is a perfect 52 x 24 foot rectangle. The projecting two-car garage with its cupola and traditionally sloped roof, adds immeasurably to the exterior appeal. The double front doors are sheltered by the covered porch. Inside, there is a wealth of livability. Two full baths, located back-to-back for plumbing economy, service the three bedrooms.

Design 31107   1,416 Sq. Ft.; 14,755 Cu. Ft.

● A smart looking traditional adaptation which, because of its perfectly rectangular shape, will be most economical to build. The low-pitched roof has a wide overhang which accentuates its low-slung qualities. The attached two-car garage is oversized to permit the location of extra bulk storage space. Further, its access to the house is through the handy separate laundry area. This house will function as either a four bedroom home, or as one that has three bedrooms, plus a quiet study. Features include a fireplace in the living room, built-in china cabinet in the breakfast room, sizable vanity in the main bath and more.

Design 31803

1,434 Sq. Ft.; 28,552 Cu. Ft.

● The texture of brick does much to enhance the beauty of this pleasing traditional home. The center entrance with its double doors is protected by the covered porch. Traffic will flow easily and efficiently. The end-living room will be free of annoying cross-room traffic. A centered fireplace wall with end book shelves is an outstanding feature of this area. The separate dining room is ideally located between the living room and kitchen which allows for its maximum use.

Design 31374 1,248 Sq. Ft.; 25,336 Cu. Ft.

● A low-pitched, overhanging roof that hugs the ground and gives an impression that belies the actual dimensions of the home is a feature of this design. Board and batten siding, stone veneer, muntined windows and paneled shutters are all earmarks of Early American styling. Planning is open and pleasant; the living area leads to the dining space and through sliding glass doors to the outdoor terrace; the in-line kitchen leads to the all-purpose family room.

OPTIONAL NO BASEMENT PLAN

Design 32597 *1,515 Sq. Ft.; 32,000 Cu. Ft.*

● Whether it be a starter house you are after, or one in which to spend your retirement years, this pleasing frame home will provide a full measure of pride in ownership. The contrast of vertical and horizontal lines, the double front doors and the coach lamp post at the garage create an inviting exterior. The floor plan functions in an orderly and efficient manner. The 26 foot gathering room has a delightful view of the rear yard and will take care of those formal dining occasions. There are two full baths serving the three bedrooms. There are plenty of storage facilities, two sets of glass doors to the terraces, a fireplace in the gathering room, a basement and an attached two-car garage to act as a buffer against the wind. A delightful home, indeed.

OPTIONAL EXTERIORS & PLANS . . .

as highlighted in this section offer a fine study in the interchangeability of varying exterior styles on a given floor plan. Occasionally one's enthusiasm for a favorite floor plan may not be matched by a similar feeling about that plan's exterior styling. Further, within one's family, members may differ about their style preferences. Here are a variety of floor plans which offer an excellent opportunity to observe how (with minor modifications) that particular plan can have differently styled exteriors. As you study these plans which range in size from 1344-1880 sq. ft. note the fine proportion and detailing of the Traditional, Contemporary, Tudor and French exteriors.

● Here is a unique series of designs with three charming exterior adaptations-Southern Colonial, Western Ranch, French Provincial - and two distinctive floor plans. Each plan has a different design number and is less than 1,600 square feet.

If yours is a preference for the floor plan featuring the 26 foot keeping room, you should order blueprints for Design 32611. Of course, the details for each of the three delightful exteriors will be included. On the other hand, should the plan with the living, dining and family rooms be your favorite, order blueprints for Design 32612 and get details for all three exteriors.

There are many points of similarity in the two designs. Each has a fireplace, 2½ baths, sliding glass doors to the rear terrace, master bedroom with walk-in closet and private bath with stall shower and a basement. It is interesting to note that two of the exteriors have covered porches. Don't miss the beamed ceilings, the various storage facilities and the stall showers.

Design 32611
1,557 Sq. Ft.; 26,245 Cu. Ft.

Design 32612
1,571 Sq. Ft.; 32,880 Cu. Ft.

Design 32802
1,729 Sq. Ft.; 42,640 Cu. Ft.

● The three exteriors shown at the left house the same, efficiently planned one-story floor plan shown below. Be sure to notice the design variations in the window placement and roof pitch. The Tudor design to the left is delightful. Half-timbered stucco and brick comprise the facade of this English Tudor variation of the plan. Note authentic bay window in the front bedroom.

Design 32803
1,679 Sq. Ft.; 36,755 Cu. Ft.

● Housed in varying facades, this floor plan is very efficient. The front foyer leads to each of the living areas. The sleeping area of two, or optional three, bedrooms is ready to serve the family. Then there is the gathering room. This room is highlighted by its size, 16 x 20 feet. A contemporary mix of fieldstone and vertical wood siding characterizes this exterior. The absence of columns or posts gives a modern look to the covered porch.

Design 32804
1,674 Sq. Ft.; 35,465 Cu. Ft.

● Stuccoed arches, multi-paned windows and a gracefully sloped roof accent the exterior of this Spanish-inspired design. Like the other two designs, the interior kitchen will efficiently serve the dining room, covered dining porch and breakfast room with great ease. Blueprints for all three designs include details for an optional non-basement plan.

OPTIONAL NON-BASEMENT

Design 32805
1,547 Sq. Ft.; 40,880 Cu. Ft.

● Three completely different exterior facades share one compact, practical and economical floor plan. The major design variations are roof pitch, window placement and garage openings. Each design will hold its own when comparing the three exteriors. The design to the right is a romantic stone-and-shingle cottage design. This design, along with the other two designs presented here, is outstanding.

Design 32806
1,584 Sq. Ft.; 41,880 Cu. Ft.

● Even though these exteriors are extremely different in their styling and also have a few design variations, their floor plans are identical. Each will provide the family with a livable plan. In this brick and half-timbered stucco Tudor version, like the other two, the living-dining room expands across the rear of the plan and has direct access to the covered porch. Notice the built-in planter adjacent to the open staircase leading to the basement.

Design 32807
1,576 Sq. Ft.; 35,355 Cu. Ft.

● Along with the living-dining areas of the other two plans, this sleek contemporary styled home's breakfast room also will have a view of the covered porch. A desk, snack bar and mud room housing the laundry facilities are near the U-shaped kitchen. Clustering these work areas together is very convenient. The master bedroom has a private bath.

OPTIONAL NON-BASEMENT

Design 32565
1,540 Sq. Ft.; 33,300 Cu. Ft.

● This modest sized floor plan has much to offer in the way of livability. It may function as either a two or three bedroom home. The living room is huge and features a fine, raised hearth fireplace. The open stairway to the basement is handy and will lead to what may be developed as the recreation area. In addition to the two full baths, there is an extra wash room. Adjacent is the laundry room and the service entrance from the garage. The blueprints you order for this design will show details for each of the three delightful elevations above. Which is your favorite? The Tudor, the Colonial or the Contemporary?

Design 32505
1,366 Sq. Ft.; 29,329 Cu. Ft.

● This design offers you a choice of three distinctively different exteriors. Which is your favorite? Blueprints show details for all three optional elevations. A study of the floor plan reveals a fine measure of livability. In less than 1,400 square feet there are features galore. An excellent return on your construction dollar. In addition to the two eating areas and the open planning of the gathering room, the indoor-outdoor relationships are of great interest. The basement may be developed for recreational activities. Be sure to note the storage potential, particularly the linen closet, the pantry, the china cabinet and the broom closet.

Design 31305 1,382 Sq. Ft.; 16,584 Cu. Ft.

● Order blueprints for any one of the three exteriors shown on this page and you will receive details for building this outstanding floor plan. You'll find the appeal of these exteriors difficult to beat. As for the plan, in less than 1,400 square feet there are three bedrooms, two full baths, a separate dining room, a formal living room, a fine kitchen overlooking the rear yard and an informal family room. In addition, there is the attached two-car garage. Note the location of the stairs when this plan is built with a basement. Each of the exteriors is predominantly brick - the front of Design 31305 (above) features both stone and vertical boards and battens with brick on the other three sides. Observe the double front doors of the French design, 31382 (below) and the Contemporary design, 31383 (bottom). Study the window treatment.

Design 31382
1,382 Sq. Ft.; 17,164 Cu. Ft.

Design 31383
1,382 Sq. Ft.; 15,448 Cu. Ft.

Design 31307 1,357 Sq. Ft.; 14,476 Cu. Ft.

● These three stylish exteriors have the same practical, L-shaped floor plan. Design 31307 (above) features a low-pitched, wide-overhanging roof, a pleasing use of horizontal siding and brick and an enclosed front flower court. Design 31380 (below) has its charm characterized by the pediment gables, the effective window treatment and the masses of brick. Design 31381 (bottom) is captivating because of its hip-roof, its dentils, panelled shutters and lamp post. Each of these three designs has a covered front porch. Inside, there is an abundance of livability. The formal living and dining area is spacious, and the U-shaped kitchen is efficient. There is informal eating space, a separate laundry and a fine family room. Note the sliding glass doors to the terrace. The blueprints include details for building either with or without a basement. Observe the pantry of the non-basement plan.

Design 31380
1,399 Sq. Ft.; 17,937 Cu. Ft.

Design 31381
1,399 Sq. Ft.; 17,937 Cu. Ft.

31

Design 31938 1,428 Sq. Ft.; 29,702 Cu. Ft.

● An efficient plan designed to fit each of the three delightful exteriors above. You can reserve your choice of exterior until you receive the blueprints. Each set you order contains the details for the construction of all three. Note the differences in exterior materials, window treatment, car storage facilities and roof lines. Observe the beamed ceiling, all purpose family room and the kitchen eating space. There is a lot of living in 1,428 square feet.

Design 31323 1,344 Sq. Ft.; 17,472 Cu. Ft.

● Incorporated in the set of blueprints for this design are details for building each of the three charming, traditional exteriors. Each of the three alternate exteriors has a distinction all its own. A study of the floor plan reveals fine livability. There are two full baths, a fine family room, an efficient work center, a formal dining area, bulk storage facilities and sliding glass doors to the quiet and living terraces. Laundry is strategically located near the kitchen.

Three Distinctively Styled Exteriors . . .

Design 32705 1,746 Sq. Ft.; 37,000 Cu. Ft.

Design 32706 1,746 Sq. Ft.; 36,800 Cu. Ft.

. . . One Practical, Efficient Floor Plan

● Three different exteriors! But inside it's all the same livable house. Begin with the impressive entry hall . . . more than 19' long and offering double entry to the gathering room. Now the gathering room which is notable for its size and design. Notice how the fireplace is flanked by sliding glass doors leading to the terrace! That's unusual.

There's a formal dining room, too! The right spot for special birthday dinners as well as supper parties for friends. And an efficient kitchen that makes meal preparation easy whatever the occasion. Look for a built-in range and oven here . . . plus a bright dining nook with sliding doors to a second terrace. Three large bedrooms! All lo-

cated to give family members the utmost privacy. Including a master suite with a private dressing room, bath and a sliding glass door opening onto the main terrace. For blueprints of the hip-roof French adaptation on the opposite page order 32705. For the Contemporary version order 32706. The Colonial order 32704.

Design 32704 1,746 Sq. Ft.; 38,000 Cu. Ft.

Design 31389
1,488 Sq. Ft.; 18,600 Cu. Ft.

● Your choice of exterior goes with this outstanding floor plan. If your tastes include a liking for French Provincial, Design 31389, above, will provide a lifetime of satisfaction. On the other hand, should you prefer the simple straightforward lines of comtemporary design, the exterior for Design 31387, below, will be your favorite. For those who enjoy the warmth of Colonial adaptations, the charming exterior for Design 31388, bottom, will be perfect. Of interest, is a comparison of these three exteriors. Observe the varying design treatment of the windows, the double front doors, the garage doors and the roof lines. Don't miss other architectural details. Study each exterior and the floor plan carefully. Three charming designs you won't want to miss.

Design 31387
1,488 Sq. Ft.; 16,175 Cu. F

Design 31388
1,488 Sq. Ft.; 18,600 Cu. Ft.

Design 31864
1,598 Sq. Ft.; 27,611 Cu. Ft.

● What's your favorite exterior? The one above which has a distinctive colonial appearance, or that below with its sleek contemporary look? Maybe you prefer the more formal hip-roof exterior (bottom) with its French feeling. Whatever your choice, you'll know your next home will be one that is delightfully proportioned and is sure to be among the most attractive in the neighborhood. It is interesting to note that each exterior highlights an effective use of wood siding and stone (or brick, as in the case of Design 31866). The floor plan features three bedrooms, 2½ baths, a formal living and dining room, a snack bar and a mud room. The master bedroom of the contemporary design has its window located in the left side elevation wall.

Design 31865
1,598 Sq. Ft.; 25,626 Cu. Ft.

Design 31866
1,598 Sq. Ft.; 27,248 Cu. Ft.

Design 32810
3-Bedroom Plan

Design 32814
4-Bedroom Plan

1,536 Sq. Ft.; 34,560 Cu. Ft.

OPTIONAL CRAWL SPACE PLAN

OPTIONAL FRONT ENTRANCE GARAGE

● 2 x 6 stud wall construction front and center! The designs on these two pages are particularly energy-efficient minded. All exterior walls employ the use of the larger size stud (in preference to the traditional 2 x 4 stud) to permit the installation of extra thick insulation. The high cornice design also allows for more ceiling insulation. In addition to the insulation factor, 2 x 6 studs are practical from an economic standpoint. According to many experts, the use of 2 x 6's spaced 24 inches O.C. results in the need for less lumber and saves construction time. However, the energy-efficient features of this series do not end with the basic framing members. Efficiency begins right at the front door where the vestibule acts as an airlock restricting the flow of cold air to the interior. The basic rectangular shape of the house spells efficiency. No complicated and costly construction here. Yet, there has been no sacrifice of delightful exterior appeal. Efficiency and economy are also embodied in such features as back-to-back plumbing, centrally located furnace, minimal window and door openings and, most important of all - size.

Design 32811
3-Bedroom Plan

Design 32815
4-Bedroom Plan

1,581 Sq. Ft.; 36,694 Cu. Ft.

Design 32812
3-Bedroom Plan

Design 32816
4-Bedroom Plan

1,581 Sq. Ft.; 35,040 Cu. Ft.

OPTIONAL CRAWL SPACE FLOOR PLAN

OPTIONAL FRONT ENTRANCE GARAGE

Within 1,536 square feet there is outstanding livability and a huge variety of options from which to choose. For instance, of the four stylish exteriors, which is your favorite? The cozy, front porch Farmhouse adaptation; the pleasing Southern Colonial version, the French creation, or the rugged Western facade? Further, do you prefer a three or a four bedroom floor plan? With or without a basement? Front or side-opening garage? If you wish to order blueprints for the hip-roofed design with three bedrooms, specify Design 32812; for the four bedroom option specify 32816. To order blueprints for the three bedroom Southern Colonial, request Design 32811; for the four bedroom model, ask for Design 32815, etc. All blueprints include the optional non-basement and front opening garage details. Whatever the version you select, you and your family will enjoy the beamed ceiling of the family room, the efficient, U-shaped kitchen, the dining area, the traffic-free living room and the fine storage facilities. Truly, a fine design series created to give each home buyer the maximum amount of choice and flexibility.

Design 32813
3-Bedroom Plan

Design 32817
4-Bedroom Plan

1,536 Sq. Ft.; 33,334 Cu. Ft.

Design 32824
1,550 Sq. Ft.; 34,560 Cu. Ft.

● Low-maintenance and economy in building are the outstanding exterior features of this sharp, one-story design. It is sheathed in long-lasting cedar siding and trimmed with stone for an eye-appealing facade. Entrance to this home takes you through a charming garden courtyard. Then through a covered walk to the front porch. The garage, extending from the front of the house, serves two purposes; to reduce lot size and to buffer the interior of the house from street noise. Sliding glass doors are featured in each of the main rooms for easy access to the outdoors. A sun porch is tucked between the study and gathering rooms. Optional non-basement details are included with the purchase of this design.

Design 32825
1,584 Sq. Ft.; 37,215 Cu. Ft.

● With today's tight economy, this house will be a real bargain. It has all of the necessary features to insure gracious living yet keep costs down - generous living space, packed with amenities and constructed with durable materials. Locating the garage to the front of this design is practical because it makes the overall width only 51' so it will fit on a narrow lot and it will act as a buffer against street noise. The interior of this home will be interesting. Three sets of sliding glass doors at the rear of the plan will flood the interior with natural light. Since it is a modified open plan it will allow the sunlight to penetrate deep into the interior. The gathering room which seems expanded by the cathedral ceiling has a fireplace.

OPTIONAL NON-BASEMENT

Design 31322 1,478 Sq. Ft.; 28,969 Cu. Ft.

Design 31321
1,478 Sq. Ft.
30,447 Cu. Ft.

Design 31320
1,478 Sq. Ft.
27,195 Cu. Ft.

● Three totally different front elevations have the same basic floor plan layout. There is a separate set of blueprints for each attractive front exterior. The economically built plan, because of its simplicity, is outstanding.

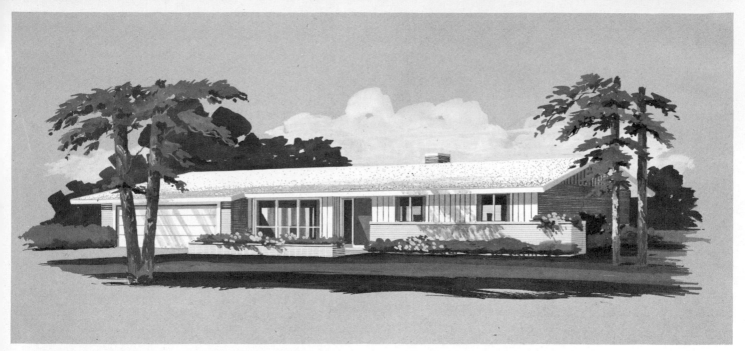

Design 31352 1,592 Sq. Ft.; 29,554 Cu. Ft.

Design 31351
1,592 Sq. Ft.
31,328 Cu. Ft.

Design 31350
1,592 Sq. Ft.
29,855 Cu. Ft.

● When you order blueprints for the exterior that appeals to you the most, you'll receive details for building with or without a basement. Note the family room and the arrangements of the two full baths.

Design 31946 1,632 Sq. Ft.; 18,931 Cu. Ft.

● Here is a delightful one-story home with a most unusual, yet appealing shape. The projecting elements add that extra measure of appeal that contributes so much to individuality. Interestingly enough, this basic exterior may have two different floor plans. If you wish blueprints for the three bedroom home order Design 31945: for four bedroom blueprints, order Design 31946. Whichever you select, you will enjoy the efficiency of the remainder of the plan. There are formal living and dining rooms, an informal family room with a beamed ceiling, a U-shaped kitchen and a strategically placed mud room with an adjacent powder room for easy convenience.

Design 31945
1,568 Sq. Ft.; 18,188 Cu. Ft.

Design 31947 1,764 Sq. Ft.; 18,381 Cu. Ft.

● When it comes to housing your family, if you are among the contemporary-minded, you'll want to give this L-shaped design a second, then even a third, or fourth, look. It is available as either a three or four bedroom home. If you desire the three bedroom, 58 foot wide design order blueprints for 31947; for the four bedroom, 62 foot wide design, order 31948. Inside, you will note a continuation of the contemporary theme with sloping ceilings, exposed beams and a practical 42 inch high storage divider between the living and dining rooms. Don't miss the mud rooms.

Design 31948
1,876 Sq. Ft.; 19,886 Cu. Ft.

Design 31331
1,880 Sq. Ft.; 21,429 Cu. Ft.

● Here is a heap of living which will fit within the confines of a relatively narrow building site. The front projecting two-car garage and the rear projecting master bedroom allow this outstanding home to be located on a much smaller, and often times less expensive, piece of property than as if the plan were a long rectangle. However, should you wish to build on a couple of acres, don't despair. The delightful exterior still will be a showplace, and the efficient floor plan will remain just as practical and livable. Blueprints for this design include details for both the optional basement and optional hip-roof elevation below. Which do you prefer?

TRADITIONAL DESIGNS

1600-2000 Sq. Ft. . . . *expand upon the exterior design impact and the livability offered by the designs featured on earlier pages. Here, are homes for the expanded building budget. Whether U-shaped, L-shaped, rectangular, or angular their floor plans offer a fine measure of complete livability for the growing family. Formal and informal living and dining capabilities are provided by the family rooms, living rooms, breakfast rooms, snack bars, and separate dining rooms. Mud room areas highlight laundries and washrooms. Master bedrooms have their private baths. The rear living areas function through sliding glass doors with their outdoor living areas. Truly fine livability.*

Design 32672 1,717 Sq. Ft.; 37,167 Cu. Ft.

● The traditional appearance of this one-story is emphasized by its covered porch, multi-paned windows, narrow clapboard and vertical wood siding. Not only is the exterior eye-appealing but the interior has an efficient plan and is very livable. The front U-shaped kitchen will work with the breakfast room and mud room, which houses the laundry facilities. An access to the garage is here. Outdoor dining can be enjoyed on the covered porch adjacent to the dining room. Both of these areas, the porch and dining room, are convenient to the kitchen. Sleeping facilities consist of three bedrooms and two full baths. Note the three sets of sliding glass doors leading to the terrace.

47

Design 31337
1,606 Sq. Ft.; 31,478 Cu. Ft.

● A pleasantly traditional facade which captures a full measure of warmth. Its exterior appeal results from a symphony of such features as: the attractive window detailing; the raised planter; the paneled door, carriage light and cupola of the garage; the use of both horizontal siding and brick. The floor plan has much to recommend this design to the family whose requirements include formal and informal living areas. There is an exceptional amount of livability in this modest-sized design.

Design 31890
1,628 Sq. Ft.; 20,350 Cu. Ft.

● The pediment gable and columns help set the charm of this modestly sized home. Here is graciousness normally associated with homes twice its size. The pleasant symmetry of the windows and the double front doors complete the picture. Inside, each square foot is wisely planned to assure years of convenient living. There are three bedrooms, each with twin wardrobe closets. There are two full baths economically grouped with the laundry and heating equipment. A fine feature.

Design 31920
1,600 Sq. Ft.; 18,966 Cu. Ft.

● A charming exterior with a truly great floor plan. The front entrance with its covered porch seems to herald all the outstanding features to be found inside. Study the sleeping zone with its three bedrooms and two full baths. Each of the bedrooms has its own walk-in closet. Note the efficient U-shaped kitchen with the family and dining rooms to each side. Observe the laundry and the extra wash room. Blueprints for this design include details for both basement and non-basement construction.

Design 32265 1,861 Sq. Ft.; 36,888 Cu. Ft.

● Inside and outside this home will provide a lifetime of satisfaction for its occupants. Whether called upon to serve the family's needs as a two or three bedroom home, it will do so with great merit. As a two bedroom home, there is then a quiet study with built-in desk, cabinets and book shelves. The front-to-rear living room is 23 feet long and functions through sliding glass doors right out into the terrace. Around the corner from the fireplace is the formal dining room. It, too, but a step from the terrace. The in-line kitchen will be efficient and function with breakfast nook. Note built-in china cabinets, pantry, wood box, vanity, linen storage and basement.

Design 32210
1,658 Sq. Ft.; 22,804 Cu. Ft.

● Certainly a unique adaptation of an Early American farm. Projecting from the main portion of the house are the living and garage wings. Anyone wishing to build an expansible house would find this design of interest. The main section of the house comprised of the bedroom, kitchen and family room areas would function ideally as the initial basic unit. Later, as the need arose, the spacious living-dining wing could be added. Then the two-car garage could be built.

50

Design 32327
1,820 Sq. Ft.; 26,897 Cu. Ft.

● You will have fun deciding which orientation on your site you most prefer for this brick veneer home. Its angular shape provides just the right touch to assure an air of distinction. The center foyer routes traffic effectively. There is no unnecessary cross-room traffic in this design. The living room with access to the rear privacy porch features an appealing raised hearth fireplace wall. Acting as a divider between the nook and family room is a counter with cabinets above and below. A pass-thru provides direct access to each room. Should you wish, you may opt to have the family room function as the dining room. The built-in planter is an attractive highlight.

Design 31044
1,904 Sq. Ft.; 37,280 Cu. Ft.

● The impact of delightful design manifests itself in many different forms and numerous divergent styles. Here is a home that is a simple rectangle with a virtually square garage which go together to result in an interesting L-shape. The charming traditional styling is characterized by the window and door treatment, the horizontal and vertical siding, the roof masses and, above all, pleasing proportion. Inside there is a simple, straight-forward, plan.

Design 31862
1,700 Sq. Ft.; 26,151 Cu. Ft.

● This impressive L-shaped traditional will be welcomed wherever built. Its exterior appeal emanates from its pleasing proportions. The spacious drive court leads to the inviting double front doors which are recessed. Inside there are the formal living and dining rooms, the informal family room and the outstanding kitchen where there is plenty of cabinet and counter space. Note the fireplace, barbecue and wash room. Observe the three bedroom, two full bath sleeping zone. Count the closets.

Design 31919
1,752 Sq. Ft.; 20,148 Cu. Ft.

● Here is a real charmer and one which your large family will have fun living in for years to come. All the facilities are present to assure convenient living. There are four good sized bedrooms. Two full back-to-back baths service the sleeping area efficiently and economically. There is the wonderfully spacious L-shaped living and dining area which looks out upon the rear terrace through sliding glass doors. The kitchen is ideally located between the dining and family rooms.

53

Design 31758
1,872 Sq. Ft.; 20,878 Cu. Ft.

● Setting the delightful character of this L-shaped traditional one-story home are such design features as: the wood columns of the covered front porch; the pediment, gabled ends; the attractive window treatment and the front entrance detail. The floor plan is an exceptional one. The nicely sized formal entry hall routes traffic ideally to the major areas of the house. The two large living areas - the informal family-kitchen and the quiet, formal living room - look out upon the rear terrace through sliding glass doors. The work center is efficient.

Design 31346
1,644 Sq. Ft.; 19,070 Cu. Ft.

● Whether you enter through the service door of the attached garage, or through the centered front entry your appreciation of what this plan has to offer will grow. The mud room area is certainly an outstanding feature. Traffic flows from this area to the informal family room with its fireplace and access to the rear terrace.

Design 31949
1,992 Sq. Ft.; 23,764 Cu. Ft.

● Surely a prize winner. Whether the contest be to pick the best in exterior appeal, or the finest in true livability, this L-shaped home will score at the top. The curving drive is a charming approach to the inviting front doors of the center entrance. The traditionally styled windows, the cupola, the contrasting materials of masonry and wood (or make it aluminum, if you prefer), the interesting roof lines and the excellent proportions are the exterior features which catch the eye. Inside, the highlights are, indeed, numerous. Of particular interest is the family room and the living room. Both are sunken to a depth of two steps, are free from traffic and look out upon the rear yard. That is a beamed ceiling in the family room.

● The paneled, front door, flanked by attractive vertical glass panels, will welcome callers to this traditional exterior with a refreshingly different floor plan. The highlight of the interior is the unique location of the family room. While it functions conveniently with the kitchen, it is also easily accessible from the front entry hall, the attached two-car garage and the covered, rear porch. A raised hearth fireplace, snack bar and sliding glass doors are plus features of this multi-purpose area. The strategic location of the extra washroom will reduce thru-the-house traffic from the outdoors. Spaciousness, resulting from the open planning of the formal living and dining rooms, permits the creation of a most gracious atmosphere.

Design 31317
1,930 Sq. Ft.; 23,573 Cu. Ft.

Design 31100
1,752 Sq. Ft.; 34,304 Cu. Ft.

● This modest sized, brick veneer home has a long list of things in its favor—from its appealing exterior to its feature-packed interior. All of the elements of its exterior complement each other to result in a symphony of attractive design features. The floor plan features three bedrooms, two full baths, an extra wash room, a family room, kitchen eating space, a formal dining area, two sets of sliding glass doors to the terrace and one set to the covered porch, built-in cooking equipment, a pantry and vanity with twin lavatories. Further, there is the living room fireplace, attached two-car garage with a bulk storage unit and a basement for extra storage and miscellaneous recreational activities. A fine investment.

Design 31343
1,620 Sq. Ft.; 18,306 Cu. Ft.

● This is truly a prize-winner! The traditional, L-shaped exterior with its flower court and covered front porch is picturesque, indeed. The formal front entry routes traffic directly to the three distinctly zoned areas—the quiet sleeping area; the spacious; formal living and dining area; the efficient, informal family-kitchen. A closer look at the floor plan reveals four bedrooms, two full baths, good storage facilities, a fine snack bar and sliding glass doors to the rear terrace. The family-kitchen is ideally located. In addition to being but a few steps from both front and rear entrances, one will enjoy the view of both yards. Blueprints include basement and non-basement details.

Design 31896
1,690 Sq. Ft.; 19,435 Cu. Ft.

● Complete family livability is provided by this exceptional floor plan. Further, this design has a truly delightful traditional exterior. The fine layout features a center entrance hall with storage closet in addition to the wardrobe closet. Then, there is the formal, front living room and the adjacent, separate dining room. The U-shaped kitchen has plenty of counter and cupboard space. There is even a pantry. The family room functions with the kitchen and is but a step from the outdoor terrace. The mud room has space for storage and laundry equipment. The extra wash room is nearby. The large family will find those four bedrooms and two full baths just the answer to sleeping and bath accommodations.

Design 31325
1,942 Sq. Ft.; 35,384 Cu. Ft.

● The large front entry hall permits direct access to the formal living room, the sleeping area and the informal family room. Both of the living areas have a fireplace. When formal dining is the occasion of the evening the separate dining room is but a step from the living room. The U-shaped kitchen is strategically flanked by the family room and the breakfast areas.

Design 32316
2,000 Sq. Ft.; 25,242 Cu. Ft.

● If you are looking for a four bedroom version of the two other designs on this page, look no further. Here, in essentially the same number of square feet, is a Colonial adaptation for a larger family. The floor planning of this basic design results in excellent zoning. The four bedroom, two-bath sleeping zone comprises a wing of its own directly accessible from the main foyer.

Design 31748
1,986 Sq. Ft.; 23,311 Cu. Ft.

● A sunken living room, two fireplaces, 2½ baths, a rear family room, a formal dining room, a mud room and plenty of storage facilities are among the features of this popular design. Blueprints include optional basement details.

OPTIONAL BASEMENT

59

Design 31130
1,856 Sq. Ft.; 36,044 Cu. Ft.

● A delightfully impressive and formal ranch home. The brick veneer, the ornamental iron columns supporting the overhanging gable, the window treatment and the cupola are among the features that contribute to the charm of this almost perfectly rectangular home. A study of the floor plan reveals excellent room relationships. The formal areas, the living and dining rooms, are adjacent to each other and overlook the front yard. The efficient kitchen is flanked by the informal breakfast area and the all-purpose family room.

Design 31091
1,666 Sq. Ft.; 28,853 Cu. Ft.

● What could be finer than to live in a delightfully designed home with all the charm of the exterior carried right inside. The interior points of interest are many. However, the focal point will surely be the family-kitchen. The work center is U-shaped and most efficient. The family activity portion of the kitchen features an attractive fireplace which will contribute to a feeling of warmth and fellowship. Nearby is the wash room and stairs to the basement.

CHINA

DINING RM.

CL. — DN. — CL.

OPTIONAL BASEMENT

TERRACE

| LIVING RM. 13⁶ x 19⁴ | DINING RM. 11⁸ x 12⁰ | KIT. 8⁰ x 12⁰ | FAMILY RM. 12⁰ x 19⁴ | STORAGE |

CHINA

HTR. CL.

RANGE

ENTRY

VANITY BATH W. D.

BATH

LIN.

CL. CL. LIN.

BED RM. 10⁰ x 10⁸

PORCH

GARAGE 19⁴ x 23⁴

CL. CL. CL.

BED RM. 13⁶ x 13⁰

BED RM. 13⁶ x 10⁴

FENCE

68'-0"
48'-0"
20'-0"
44'-0"

Design 31385 1,632 Sq. Ft.; 19,384 Cu. Ft.

● The charm of this colonial home is to be found in its appealing proportion and its outstanding window details. The wood fence with its lamp post helps create an inviting court adjacent to the covered front entrance. A study of the floor plan reveals excellent zoning. The efficient kitchen functions ideally with the family room which opens onto the outdoor terrace through sliding glass doors. Conveniently located between the quiet living room and the kitchen is the separate dining room. It, too, opens onto the terrace. Blueprints for this design include basement details.

DINING DN.

KITCHEN

CL. REF'G

ENTRY

CL. CL.

OPTIONAL BASEMENT

TERRACE

| LIVING RM. 25⁴ x 15⁰ | DINING | FAMILY-KITCHEN 14⁰ x 19⁴ | GARAGE 18⁶ x 23⁴ |

BED RM. 10⁰ x 10⁴

AIR COND.

W. D.

SNACKS

PANTRY

CL.

ENTRY

REF'G S. D.W. RANGE

BED RM. 10⁰ x 10⁰

VANITY BATH

BATH

LIN.

CL. CL.

CL. CL.

PORCH

BED RM. 13⁴ x 10⁸

MASTER BED RM. 11⁸ x 14⁸

60'-0"
26'-0"
33'-2"
50'-10"
24'-0"
26'-0"

Design 31384 1,636 Sq. Ft.; 18,536 Cu. Ft.

● Here, a wise and economical use of space results in a most practical plan with exceptional livability. There are four bedrooms, two full baths, a 25-foot formal living and dining area, a wonderful family kitchen, an attached two-car garage and a covered front porch. For those who wish to build with a basement there is the optional plan included with the blueprints. Features that are particularly noteworthy are the private bath for the master bedroom, the twin lavatories for the main bath, the island snack bar of the kitchen, the extra closets and the pantry in the kitchen.

Design 31829
1,800 Sq. Ft.; 32,236 Cu. Ft.

● All the charm of a traditional heritage is wrapped up in this U-shaped home with its narrow, horizontal siding, delightful window treatment and high-pitched roof. The massive center chimney, the bay window and the double front doors are plus features. Inside, the living potential is outstanding. The sleeping wing is self-contained and has four bedrooms and two baths. The large family and living rooms cater to the divergent age groups.

Design 31980
1,901 Sq. Ft.; 36,240 Cu. Ft.

● Planned for easy living, the daily living patterns of the active family will be pleasant ones, indeed. All the elements are present to assure a wonderful family life. The impressive exterior is enhanced by the recessed front entrance area with its covered porch. The center entry results in a convenient and efficient flow of traffic. A secondary entrance leads from the covered side porch, or the garage, into the first floor laundry. Note the powder room nearby.

Design 32360
1,936 Sq. Ft.; 37,026 Cu. Ft.

● There is no such thing as taking a fleeting glance at this charming home. Fine proportion and pleasing lines assure a long and rewarding study. Inside, the family's everyday routine will enjoy all the facilities which will surely guarantee pleasurable living. Note the sunken living room with its fireplace flanked by storage cabinets and book shelves. Observe the excellent kitchen just a step from the dining room and the nook.

Design 31252
1,985 Sq. Ft.; 24,924 Cu. ft.

● Here is a traditional adaptation which embodies all the warmth and appeal to make its occupants swell with pride. The projection of the bedroom wing, the recessed front entrance, the boxed bay windows and the set-back attached two-car garage all contribute to the interesting lines of the front exterior. The floor plan is one which contains all the features an active family would require to assure years of exceptional livability. There are two full baths in the three bedroom sleeping area, a sunken formal living room, a separate dining room and a spacious rear family room.

Design 32550
1,892 Sq. Ft.; 39,590 Cu. Ft.

● An enchanting low-slung traditional ranch with exceptional appeal. The low-pitched roof has a wide overhang and exposed beams. Stone and vertical siding offer a pleasing contrast. However, you may wish to substitute other materials of your choice. The diamond lite windows, the fence with its lamp post, the double front doors and the dovecote above the carriage lamp of the garage are among the interesting exterior features. Inside, there are four bedrooms and two full baths in the sleeping wing. The L-shaped living area is spacious and features a sloping ceiling for the gathering and dining rooms. The open stairwell to the basement recreation area is attractive. The pleasant kitchen is flanked by the nook and laundry.

Design 31186
1,872 Sq. Ft.; 31,680 Cu. Ft.

● This appealing home has an interesting and practical floor plan. It is cleverly zoned to cater to the living patterns of both the children and the parents. The children's bedroom wing projects to the rear and functions with their informal family room. The master bedroom is ideally isolated and is located in a part of the plan's quietly formal wing. The efficient kitchen looks out upon the rear terrace and functions conveniently with the dining area and family room. A full bath serves each of the two main living areas. A built-in vanity highlights each bath. The mud room features laundry equipment, storage unit and stairs to the basement. The blueprints show details for basement and non-basement construction.

Design 33144
1,760 Sq. Ft.; 19,240 Cu. Ft.

OPTIONAL BASEMENT PLAN

● If you are short on space and searching for a home that is long on both good looks and livability, search no more! This impressive L-shaped home measures merely 56'-5" in width. It, therefore, qualifies for placement on a relatively narrow building site. Of course with land costs so high, the purchase of a smaller and less expensive building site can significantly reduce the building budget. Whether you build with, or without, a basement (blueprints include details for both types of construction) the outstanding livability remains. There are three bedrooms, two baths, a formal rear living room, a big breakfast room, an excellent kitchen, a wash room and laundry and a huge bulk storage area projecting from the front of the garage. Note window treatment.

Design 31280
1,730 Sq. Ft.; 33,837 Cu. Ft.

● This medium-sized, L-shaped ranch home with its touch of traditional styling is, indeed, pleasing to the eye. Hub of this plan is the centrally located foyer which controls traffic to the bedrooms, living/dining room and family room. Economically planned circulation spends very little floor space on hallways. Back-to-back fireplaces in the family room and the living room are an effective sound barrier between the informal and formal areas. Strategically placed kitchen allows for a convenient observation post overlooking family room. The kitchen features a snack bar, built-in desk with shelves and adjacent mud room with washroom. This design includes a basement for future development or storage space.

Design 32261
1,825 Sq. Ft.; 33,814 Cu. Ft.

● This distinctive L-shaped home virtually exudes traditional warmth and charm. And little wonder, for the architectural detailing is, indeed, exquiste. Notice the fine window detailing, the appealing cornice work, the attractiveness of the garage door and the massive chimney. The dovecote and the weathervane add to the design impact. The covered front porch shelters the entry which is strategically located to provide excellent traffic patterns. A service entry from the garage is conveniently located handy to the laundry, wash room, kitchen and stairs to the basement. The beamed ceilinged family room will naturally be everyone's favorite spot for family living.

Design 32603

1,949 Sq. Ft.; 41,128 Cu. Ft.

● Surely it would be difficult to beat the appeal of this traditional one-story home. Its slightly modified U-shape with the two front facing gables, the bay window, the covered front porch and the interesting use of exterior materials all add to the exterior charm. Besides, there are three large bedrooms serviced by two full baths and three walk-in closets. The excellent kitchen is flanked by the formal dining room and the informal family room. Don't miss the pantry, the built-in oven and the pass-thru to the snack bar. The handy first floor laundry is strategically located to act as a mud room. The extra wash room is but a few steps away. The sizable living room highlights a fireplace and a picture window. Note the location of the basement stairs.

Design 33177

1,888 Sq. Ft.; 21,264 Cu. Ft.

● It would certainly be difficult to pack more living potential into such a modestly sized home than this. The family's living patterns will be just great with "convenience" as the byword. Consider: three bedrooms serviced by two full baths; a formal living room and a formal dining room overlooking the rear terrace and free from unnecessary cross-room traffic; an interior kitchen functioning ideally with the dining room, the family room and the laundry; a powder room handy to living and family rooms and kitchen. Observe: stall shower, fireplace, abundant wardrobe closets, built-in planter, snack bar, family room storage wall and sliding glass doors. The exterior is charming.

Design 31282
1,732 Sq. Ft.; 33,913 Cu. Ft.

● If it is just good plain economical livability with an exterior that has a flair for distinction that you are seeking, you'll find this traditional home difficult to top. Within only 1,732 square feet there are all the features the average family could require, plus a few for good measure. Observe that there are two full baths with one compartmented in such a manner as to conveniently serve two distinct areas—the master bedroom and the family-kitchen. There won't be any lack of storage facilities with all that cupboard and closet space. The 21 foot living room has a fireplace and built-in book shelves. There is the formal dining room and then, the covered porch nearby for warm evening relaxation. The family-kitchen is ideal.

Design 32742
1,907 Sq. Ft.; 38,950 Cu. Ft.

● Colonial charm is expressed in this one-story design by the vertical siding, the post pillars, the cross fence, paned glass windows and the use of stone. A 19' wide living room, a sloped ceilinged family room with a raised hearth fireplace and its own terrace, a kitchen with many built-ins and a dining room with built-in china cabinets are just some of the highlights. The living terrace is accessible from the dining room and master bedroom. There are two more bedrooms and a full bath in addition to the master bedroom.

Design 31222
1,657 Sq. Ft.; 32,444 Cu. Ft.

● How will you call upon this home to function? As a three or four bedroom home? The study permits all kinds of flexibility in your living patterns. If you wish, the extra room could serve the family as a TV area or an area for sewing, hobbies or guests. The 27 foot living room features a formal dining area which is but a step from the secluded, covered dining porch and efficient kitchen. There is a strategically located mud room which houses the washer and dryer and adjacent washroom. The stairs leading to the basement are also in this area.

Design 32533
1,897 Sq. Ft.; 40,523 Cu. Ft.

● The distinctive appeal of the traditional, L-shaped ranch home is indeed, hard to beat. Particularly, one with such exquisite exterior appointments. Notice the delightful window and door treatment, the covered front porch, the vertical siding and the fieldstone, the dovecote and the carriage lamp. The center entrance with its slate floor routes traffic effectively to all areas. The four bedroom sleeping wing highlights two full baths. The formal living and dining rooms act as a buffer between sleeping area and the all-purpose family room/kitchen zone. The family room has sliding glass doors, a fireplace and a large bay window for extra informal eating space. There is a first floor laundry, an extra washroom and a basement.

Shared Expense – Shared Livability

TERRACE

MASTER BEDROOM 11⁰ x 16⁸
STUDY/BEDROOM 10⁴ x 11⁰ + BAY
COVERED PORCH
SKYLIGHT   SKYLIGHT   SKYLIGHT
STUDY/BEDROOM 10⁴ x 11⁰ + BAY
MASTER BEDROOM 11⁰ x 16⁸

GREAT RM. 24⁰ x 14¹⁰

DRESSING RM.   BATH
BATH   DRESSING RM.

FOYER
FOYER

COVERED PORCH
DINING RM. 11⁴ x 11⁸ + BAY
KITCHEN 9⁰ x 11⁸
COVERED PORCH

GARAGE 13⁴ x 22⁰
STOR.
STOR.
GARAGE 13⁴ x 22⁰

48'-8"
77'-4"

Design 32869
1,986 Sq. Ft.; 48,455 Cu. Ft.

● This traditional one-story design offers the economical benefits of shared living space without sacrificing privacy. The common area of this design is centrally located between the two private, sleeping wings. The common area, 680 square feet, is made up of the great room, dining room and kitchen. Sloping the ceiling in this area creates an open feeling as will the sliding glass doors on each side of the fireplace. These doors lead to a large covered porch with skylights above. Separate outdoor entrances lead to each of the sleeping wings. Two bedrooms, dressing area, full bath and space for an optional kitchenette occupy 653 square feet in each wing. Additional space will be found in the basement which is the full size of the common area. Don't miss the covered porch and garage with additional storage space.

ENGLISH TUDOR STYLES . . .

. . . when adapted to the one-story home can capture all the charm of its popular two-story counterpart. The low profile of the one-story can, indeed, dramatically accommodate the prudent use of simulated half-timbers, stucco, wavy-edged siding, patterned brickwork, sculptured chimneys, and diamond-paned casement windows. Supplementing the Tudors in this section are four more to be found in the Optional Elevations & Plans section. The resulting square footage range is 1540 to slightly in excess of 2000 sq. ft. Of particular interest are two designs with complete one floor livability, plus bonus space on a second floor.

Design 32170
1,646 Sq. Ft.; 22,034 Cu. Ft.

● An L-shaped home with an enchanting Olde English styling. The wavy-edged siding, the simulated beams, the diamond lite windows, the unusual brick pattern and the interesting roof lines all are elements which set the character of authenticity. The center entry routes traffic directly to the formal living and sleeping zones of the house. Between the kitchen-family room area and the attached two-car garage is the mud room. Here is the washer and dryer with the extra powder room nearby. The family room is highlighted by the beamed ceilings, the raised hearth fireplace and sliding glass doors to the rear terrace. The work center with its abundance of cupboard space will be fun in which to function. Four bedrooms, two full baths and good closet space are features of the sleeping area.

Design 32605

1,775 Sq. Ft.; 34,738 Cu. Ft.

● Here are three modified L-shaped Tudor designs with tremendous exterior appeal and efficient floor plans. While each plan features three bedrooms and 2½ baths, the square footage differences are interesting. Note that each design may be built with or without a basement. This appealing exterior is highlighted by a variety of roof planes, patterned brick, wavy-edged siding and a massive chimney. The garage is oversized and has good storage potential. In addition to the entrance court, there are two covered porches and two terraces for outdoor living. Most definitely a home to be enjoyed by all family members.

Design 32206

1,769 Sq. Ft.; 25,363 Cu. Ft.

● The charm of Tudor adaptations has become increasingly popular in recent years. And little wonder. Its freshness of character adds a unique touch to any neighborhood. This interesting one-story home will be a standout wherever you choose to have it built. The covered front porch leads to the formal front entry–the foyer. From this point traffic flows freely to the living and sleeping areas. The outstanding plan features a separate dining room, a beamed ceiling living room, an efficient kitchen and an informal family room.

OPTIONAL BASEMENT

Design 32604
1,956 Sq. Ft.; 28,212 Cu. Ft.

● A feature that will set the whole wonderful pattern of true living will be the 26 foot wide country kitchen. The spacious, L-shaped kitchen has its efficiency enhanced by the island counter work surface. Beamed ceilings, fireplace and sliding glass doors add to the cozy atmosphere of this area. The laundry, dining room and entry hall are but a step or two away. The big keeping room also has a fireplace and can function with the terrace. Observe the 2½ baths.

Design 32728
1,825 Sq. Ft.; 38,770 Cu. Ft.

● Your family's new lifestyle will surely flourish in this charming, L-shaped English adaptation. The curving front driveway produces an impressive approach. A covered front porch shelters the centered entry hall which effectively routes traffic to all areas. The fireplace is the focal point of the spacious, formal living and dining area. The kitchen is strategically placed to service the dining room and any informal eating space developed in the family room. In addition to the two full baths of the sleeping area, there is a handy washroom at the entrance from the garage. A complete, first floor laundry is nearby and has direct access to the yard. Sliding glass doors permit easy movement to the outdoor terrace and side porch. Don't overlook the basement and its potential for the development of additional livability and/or storage.

Design 32286
1,496 Sq. Ft. - First Floor
751 Sq. Ft. - Second Floor; 32,165 Cu. Ft.

● There is a touch of Tudor styling here. It houses four bedrooms, two baths and a sizable family dining room with a cozy beamed ceiling. Note access to rear terrace from both family room and nook. The front, raised planter is a delightful feature.

Design 32374
1,919 Sq. Ft.; 39,542 Cu. Ft.

● This English adaptation will never grow old. There is, indeed, much here to please the eye for many a year to come. The wavy-edged siding contrasts pleasingly with the diagonal pattern of brick below. The diamond lites of the windows create their own special effect. The projecting brick wall creates a pleasant court outside the covered front porch. The floor plan is well-zoned with the three bedrooms and two baths comprising a distinct sleeping wing. Flanking the entrance hall is the formal living room and the informal, multi-purpose family room. The large dining room is strategically located. The mud room area is adjacent to the extra washroom and the stairs to the basement.

Design 32859
1,599 Sq. Ft.; 37,497 Cu. Ft.

● Incorporated into the extremely popular basic one-story floor plan is a super-insulated structure. This means that it has double exterior walls separated by R-33 insulation and a raised roof truss that insures ceiling insulation will extend to the outer wall. More popularity is shown in the always popular Tudor facade. Enter the home through the air-locked vestibule to the foyer. To the left is the sleeping area. To the right of the foyer is the breakfast room, kitchen and stairs to the basement. Viewing the rear yard are the gathering and dining rooms. Study the technical details described in the blueprints of the wall section so you can better understand this super-insulated house.

Design 32606
1,499 Sq. Ft.; 19,716 Cu. Ft.

● This modest sized house with its 1,499 square feet could hardly offer more in the way of exterior charm and interior livability. Measuring only 60 feet in width means it will not require a huge, expensive piece of property. The orientation of the garage and the front drive court are features which promote an economical use of property. In addition to the formal, separate living and dining rooms, there is the informal kitchen/family room area. Note the beamed ceiling, the fireplace, the sliding glass doors and the eating area of the family room.

Design 32737
1,796 Sq. Ft.; 43,240 Cu. Ft.

● You will be able to build this distinctive, modified U-shaped one-story home on a relatively narrow site. But, then, if you so wished, with the help of your architect and builder you may want to locate the garage to the side of the house. Inside, the living potential is just great. The interior U-shaped kitchen handily services the dining and family rooms and nook. A rear covered porch functions ideally with the family room while the formal living room has its own terrace. Three bedrooms and two baths highlight the sleeping zone (or make it two bedrooms and a study). Notice the strategic location of the washroom, laundry, two storage closets and the basement stairs.

Design 32129

2,057 Sq. Ft.; 36,970 Cu. Ft.

● Here are two designs just slightly over 2,000 sq. ft. Their exterior charm is matched by their outstanding interior livability. The four bedroom home above is zoned for convenient living. Its sleeping area with two full baths and plenty of closets will have a lot of privacy. The formal living and dining rooms function together and may be completely by-passed when desired. Informal living areas are grouped together and overlook the rear yard. The family room with its beamed ceiling is but a step from the kitchen and terrace. The U-shaped kitchen is handy to both the breakfast and dining rooms. A first floor laundry and extra washroom are strategically located for your everyday convenience.

Design 32318

2,029 Sq. Ft.; 31,021 Cu. Ft.

● Warmth and charm are characteristics of Tudor adaptations. This home with its twin, front-facing gabled roofs represents a great investment. While it will be an exciting and refreshing addition to any neighborhood, its appeal will never grow old. The front entrance opens to the center foyer. Traffic patterns flow in an orderly and efficient manner to the three main zones - the formal dining zone, the sleeping zone and the informal living zone. The sunken living room with its fireplace is separated from the dining room by an attractive trellis divider. A second fireplace, along with beamed ceiling and sliding glass doors, highlights the family room.

Design 32127 1,712 Sq. Ft. - First Floor; 450 Sq. Ft. - Second Floor; 39,435 Cu. Ft.

● Here is a basic one-story home with three bedrooms and two full baths, plus a bonus second floor under its high pitched roof. Features are plenty - both inside and out. A list of the exterior design highlights is most interesting. It begins with the character created by the impressive roof surfaces. The U-shape creates a unique appeal and results in the formation of a front, garden court. Exterior detailing of the projecting wings is delightful, indeed. The massive chimney is worthy of particular note. Inside, the living room features a sloping, beamed ceiling. It also has space left over for the formal dining. The family room has a flat, beamed ceiling. Sleeping facilities are exceptional. Upstairs there is an optional master bedroom suite if you choose to develop this area.

Design 32277
1,903 Sq. Ft.; 25,087 Cu. Ft.

● Tudor design front and center! And what an impact this beautifully proportioned L-shaped home does deliver. Observe the two different floor plans.

OPTIONAL BASEMENT

Design 32678
1,971 Sq. Ft.; 42,896 Cu. Ft.

● This delightful Tudor design has the option of two efficient floor plans. Design 32277 has its formal and informal area broken down into a living room and a family room. Where Design 32678 has a living room and an informal area of a large country kitchen. This design also has a basement. Both plans have three bedrooms.

FRENCH FACADES . . .

in their many forms can offer a delightfully formal appearance. They are generally characterized by their trim hip roofs. Casement windows with muntins, shutters, brick quoins at the exterior corners, dentil-work, patterned doors and brick veneer exteriors are among other distinguishing features. This selection illustrates how an abundance of livability can be designed into a variety of floor plan configurations. Note the modified U-shaped plan below and variations of L-shapes and rectangles on succeeding pages. Indoor-outdoor living relationships are important as are flexible formal and informal living and dining capabilities. The private, sleeping area is well-planned in each design.

Design 32738
1,898 Sq. Ft.; 36,140 Cu. Ft.

● Impressive architectural work is indeed apparent in this three bedroom home. The three foot high entrance court wall, the high pitched roof and the paned glass windows all add to this home's exterior appeal. It is also apparent that the floor plan is very efficient with the side, U-shaped kitchen and nook with two pantry closets. Overlooking the backyard, the dining and gathering rooms will serve your every family occasion. Three (or make it two with a study) bedrooms and two baths are in the sleeping wing. Indoor-outdoor living also will be enjoyed in this home with a dining terrace off the nook and a living terrace off the gathering room and master bedroom. Note the fireplace in the gathering room and bay window in dining room. This design will be very livable.

Design 31330
1,820 Sq. Ft.; 22,207 Cu. Ft.

● A dramatic, formal exterior uses strong horizontal cornice lines to accentuate its low-slung qualities. The brick quoins at the corners, the paneled shutters, the ornamental iron and the hip-roof contribute to a distinctly continental flavor. Inside, the various areas are clearly defined. The bedrooms and living room are away from the noise of the family and service areas. The living room can double as a den-study. The U-shaped kitchen with pass-thru counters serves both the family room and dining area conveniently. The sleeping wing is highlighted by three sizable bedrooms, two baths and an abundance of wardrobe storage facilities. Optional fireplace details are included with the plan.

Design 31326
2,014 Sq. Ft.; 36,948 Cu. Ft.

● This pleasing, French Provincial adaptation has an extremely practical basic floor plan which contains many of those "extras" that contribute so much to good living. Among the features that make this such an outstanding home are: two fireplaces—one with raised hearth and wood box, first floor laundry, extra washroom, powder room, snack bar, separate dining room, partial basement, garage storage and workbench. With the four bedrooms and the formal and informal living areas, there is plenty of space in which the large family may move around and enjoy their surroundings.

Design 31892
2,036 Sq. Ft.; 26,575 Cu. Ft.

● The romance of French Provincial is captured here by the hip-roof masses, the charm of the window detailing, the brick quoins at the corners, the delicate dentil work at the cornices, the massive centered chimney and the recessed double front doors. The slightly raised entry court completes the picture. The basic floor plan is a favorite of many. And little wonder, for all areas work well together, while still maintaining a fine degree of separation of functions. The highlight of the interior, perhaps, will be the sunken living room. The family room with its beamed ceiling will not be far behind in its popularity. The separate dining room, mud room and efficient kitchen complete the livability.

Design 31797
1,618 Sq. Ft.; 18,600 Cu. Ft.

● A house to be looked at and lived in —that's what this impressively formal French Provincial adaptation represents. The front court, just inside the brick wall with its attractive iron gate, sets the patterns of formality that are so apparent inside. The formal living and dining rooms separate the sleeping area from the kitchen/family room area. A pass-thru facilitates serving of informal snacks in family room. The three bedrooms will serve the average sized family perfectly. Details for an optional basement are included with this plan.

Design 31272
1,690 Sq. Ft.; 32,588 Cu. Ft.

● Designed for the family who wants the refinement of French Provincial, but on a small scale. Keynoting its charm are the long shutters, the delightful entrance porch with its wood posts, the interesting angles of the hip roof and the pair of paneled garage doors. Behind this formal facade is a simple, efficient, up-to-date floor plan. The living patterns for the family occupying this house will be toward the rear where the long living terrace is just a step outside the glass sliding doors of the formal and informal living areas. The two bathrooms in the sleeping area share back-to-back plumbing, which is economical.

Design 31362
1,896 Sq. Ft.; 21,262 Cu. Ft.

● This dramatic L-shaped French adaptation is distinctive indeed. The projecting bedroom wing, consisting of three bedrooms, adds to the exterior appeal. Inside, the traffic patterns are excellent. The blueprints show optional basement details as well as an optional fireplace in the living room. This is most definitely a design to please all family members.

86

Design 31120
1,492 Sq. Ft.; 27,482 Cu. Ft.

● The hip roof of this design gives it a somewhat French flavor. Centered, the front entrance is recessed to provide shelter during inclement weather. A glass panel to the right of the front door permits the entry hall to enjoy plenty of natural light. Adjacent to the entry, the front kitchen, preferred by many, permits an easy view of approaching callers. The rear living and dining area measures 31 feet and looks upon the rear yard through a large window. Dining on the terrace will be most enjoyable since it will have plenty of privacy.

Design 31815
1,592 Sq. Ft.; 21,365 Cu. Ft.

● Delicately arched windows and doors, wrought iron trellis-work, paneled doors and fine cornice treatment all mark this house as reminiscent of French Provincial. The covered front porch is another feature not to be overlooked. While the L-shape of this house is a distinctive factor in contributing to the exterior design appeal, it is equally important in contributing to outstanding floor planning. Study the zoning. Note how each of the three main areas - formal living and dining, informal kitchen and family and quiet sleeping all enjoy their separation from each other.

SPANISH & WESTERN ADAPTATIONS . . .

offer a refreshing change of pace wherever they may be built. While stucco surfaces are frequently used, brick and wood siding can have their own full measure of appeal. Wide-overhanging roofs with exposed rafter tails, window and porch arches, wrought iron grillwork, splayed chimneys, and massive panelled doors are distinguishing features. Enclosed courtyards are often integrated with the plan to provide a more private front entrance. Further, the courtyard provides an additional outdoor living area to supplement the terraces generally located to the rear. Because of their low-pitched roofs, sloping, beamed ceilings are frequent interior features.

Design 32200
1,695 Sq. Ft.; 18,916 Cu. Ft.

● The two plans featured here are both housed in this L-shaped ranch home. Its exterior shows a Spanish influence by utilizing a stucco exterior finish, grilled windows and an arched entryway. Beyond the arched entryway is the private front court which leads to the tiled foyer. Interior livability has been well planned in both designs.

OPTIONAL BASEMENT PLAN

Design 32677
1,634 Sq. Ft.; 26,770 Cu. Ft.

● Notice the difference in these plan's livability. Design 32200 has a shared living dining room overlooking the backyard and a front master bedroom with a side terrace where Design 32677 has a separate front dining room, family room with access to the rear terrace and a rear master bedroom with an adjacent covered porch. Both designs have two additional bedrooms besides the master bedroom. Access to the basement varies in each plan.

Design 32741
1,842 Sq. Ft.; 37,045 Cu. Ft.

● Here is another example of what 1,800 square feet can deliver in comfort and convenience. The setting reminds one of the sun country of Arizona. However, this design would surely be an attractive and refreshing addition to any region. The covered front porch with its adjacent open trellis area shelters the center entry. From here traffic flows efficiently to the sleeping, living and kitchen zones. There is much to recommend each area. The sleeping with its fine bath and closet facilities; the living with its spaciousness, fireplace and adjacent dining room; the kitchen with its handy nook, excellent storage, nearby laundry and extra wash room.

Design 32386
1,994 Sq. Ft.; 22,160 Cu. Ft.

● This distinctive home may look like the Far West, but don't let that inhibit you from enjoying the great livability it has to offer. Wherever built, you will surely experience a satisfying pride of ownership. Imagine, an entrance court in addition to a large side courtyard! A central core is made up of the living, dining and family rooms, plus the kitchen. Each functions with an outdoor living area. The younger generation has its sleeping zone divorced from the master bedroom. The location of the attractive attached garage provides direct access to the front entry. Don't miss the vanity, the utility room with laundry equipment, the snack bar and the raised hearth fireplace. Note three pass-thrus from the kitchen. Observe the beamed and sloping ceilings of the living areas.

Design 32743
1,892 Sq. Ft.; 23,300 Cu. Ft.

● For those who feel they really don't require both a living and a family room, this refreshing contemporary will serve its occupants well, indeed. Ponder deeply its space and livability; for this design makes a lot of economic sense, too. First of all, placing the attached garage at the front cuts down on the size of a site required. It also represents an appealing design factor. The privacy wall and overhead trellis provide a pleasant front courtyard. Inside, the gathering room satisfies the family's more gregarious instincts, while there is always the study nearby to serve as a more peaceful haven. The separate dining room and the nook offer dining flexibility. The two full baths highlight the economical back-to-back plumbing feature. Note the rear terraces.

Design 32593
1,391 Sq. Ft.; 28,781 Cu. Ft.

● A fireplace wall in the gathering room includes a raised hearth and two built-in wood boxes. There is a beamed ceiling, too. Inviting warmth is in this spacious gathering room which is more than 22' x 13' with ample space for a dining area. There's a sunny breakfast room, too, with sliding glass doors leading to the terrace and a pass-through from the kitchen. For efficiency, the kitchen is U-shaped and has lots of counter space. Two full baths. Three bedrooms! Including one with a private bath and one suitable for use as a study, if that's your desire. This home is ideal for young families and equally perfect for those whose children are grown! It offers many of the attractive extras usually reserved for larger and more expensive designs. The appealing exterior will be appreciated.

Design 31088
1,408 Sq. Ft.; 14,305 Cu. Ft.

● This pleasing home will be just the one to satisfy the medium budget. You'll forever be proud of what your construction dollar bought; for you'll never tire of the attractive exterior and you'll never cease to be thankful for the fine livability of the interior. The three bedrooms are serviced by two full baths. The family's living habits will be admirably taken care of by the big, formal living room and the multi-purpose family room. The homemaker will love the front kitchen and be grateful for the pass-thru to the family room. Don't miss the built-in book storage unit, the bathroom vanity, the extra closets, the washroom and the sliding glass doors.

Design 32528
1,754 Sq. Ft.; 37,832 Cu. Ft.

● This inviting, U-shaped western ranch adaptation offers outstanding living potential behind its double, front doors and flanking glass panels. In but 1,754 square feet there are three bedrooms, 2½ baths, a formal living room and an informal family room, an excellently functioning interior kitchen, an adjacent breakfast nook and good storage facilities. The open stairwell to the lower level basement can be an interesting, interior feature. Note raised hearth fireplace and sloped ceiling.

Design 32232
1,776 Sq. Ft.; 17,966 Cu. Ft.

● This appealing, flat roof design has its roots in the Spanish Southwest. The arched, covered porch with its heavy beamed ceiling sets the note of distinction. The center foyer routes traffic effectively to the main zones of the house. Down a step is the sunken living room. Privacy will be the byword here. The cluster of three bedrooms features two full baths and good storage facilities.

Design 32557
1,955 Sq. Ft.; 43,509 Cu. Ft.

● This eye-catching design has a flavor of the Spanish Southwest. The character of the exterior is set by the wide, overhanging roof with its exposed beams; the massive, arched pillars; the arching of the brick over the windows; the panelled door and the horizontal siding that contrasts with the brick. The master bedroom/study suite is a focal point of the interior. However, if necessary, the study could become the fourth bedroom. The living and dining rooms are large and separated by a massive raised hearth fireplace.

Design 31726
1,910 Sq. Ft.; 19,264 Cu. Ft.

● The U-shaped plan has long been honored for its excellent zoning. As the floor plan for this fine Spanish adaptation illustrates, it not only provides separation between parents' area and children's wing, but also it places a buffer area in the center. This makes the kitchen the "control center" for the home - handy to the family room, living room and the dining alcove.

Design 32671
1,589 Sq. Ft.; 36,210 Cu. Ft.

● A rustic exterior of this one-story home features vertical wood siding. The entry foyer is floored with flagstone and leads to the three areas of the plan: sleeping, living and work center. The sleeping area has three bedrooms, the master bedroom has sliding glass doors to the rear terrace. The living area, consisting of gathering and dining rooms, also has access to the terrace. The work center is efficiently planned. It houses the kitchen with snack bar, breakfast room with built-in china cabinet and stairs to the basement. This is a very livable plan.

Design 32355
1,892 Sq. Ft.; 19,300 Cu. Ft.

● Whether you build this contemporary out in the country or on a relatively narrow suburban site, it will matter very little. And it will not diminish the unique livability a bit! Here in less than 1,900 square feet are four bedrooms, two living areas, a separate dining room and an outstanding kitchen. The major rooms, excluding the kitchen, have sloping ceilings. Sliding glass doors permit the bedrooms and the living and family rooms to function with the outdoor pool and terrace. Notice the raised hearth fireplace, the snack bar and the walk-in closet of the master bedroom. The utility room houses the laundry equipment.

Design 32293
2,010 Sq. Ft.; 23,014 Cu. Ft.

● This is an L-shaped court design which gives the interesting appearance of a group of cluster units. The various hipped-roof planes have a wide over-hang and an appealing raised cap. The sleeping area is a unit by itself and contains four bedrooms and two full baths. The living and dining rooms represent a delightfully spacious area with plenty of glass looking out on the rear terrace. Functioning through sliding glass doors with both the court and the side terrace, the family room with beamed ceiling has a fireplace. The garage appears to be a unit by itself, yet it is attached to the mud room with the extra washroom nearby.

Design 31754 2,080 Sq. Ft.; 21,426 Cu. Ft.

● Boasting a traditional Western flavor, this rugged U-shaped ranch home has the features to assure grand living. The front flower court, inside the high brick wall, creates a delightfully dramatic atmosphere which carries inside. The floor plan is positively unique and exceptionally livable. Wonderfully zoned, the three bedrooms enjoy their full measure of privacy. The formal living and dining rooms function together in a most pleasing fashion. The laundry, kitchen, informal eating and family room fit together to guarantee efficient living patterns.

CONTEMPORARY DESIGNS 1200-1599 Sq. Ft. . . .

offer a refreshing and exciting break from the many other so-called "high-styled" traditional exteriors. Their simple, straightforward, uncluttered appearance make contemporary exteriors a favorite of many. The houses in this section exemplify the fact that distinctive, yet practical, contemporary design can come in modest packages. Whether simple rectangles, modified L-shapes, or irregular configurations, their floor plans can deliver interesting and convenient living patterns. Whether their exteriors have a low, ground-hugging profile, a geometric shape, or an angular appearance they can capture the eye of even the most casual passer-by in a most pleasing fashion.

Design 32818 1,566 Sq. Ft.; 20,030 Cu. Ft.

● This is most certainly an outstanding contemporary design. Study the exterior carefully before your journey to inspect the floor plan. The vertical lines are carried from the siding to the paned windows to the garage door. The front entry is recessed so the overhanging roof creates a covered porch.

Note the planter court with privacy wall. The floor plan is just as outstanding. The rear gathering room has a sloped ceiling, raised hearth fireplace, sliding glass doors to the terrace and a snack bar with pass-thru to the kitchen. In addition to the gathering room, there is the living room/study. This

room could be utilized in a variety of ways depending on your family's choice. The formal dining room is convenient to the U-shaped kitchen. Three bedrooms and two closely located baths are in the sleeping wing. This plan includes details for the construction of an optional basement.

● A well-planned, medium sized contemporary home with plenty of big-house features. The brick line of the projected bedroom wing extends toward the projected two-car garage to form an attractive front court. The large glass panels below the overhanging roof are a dramatic feature. In addition to the two full baths, there is an extra wash room easily accessible from the kitchen/family room area as well as the outdoors. The laundry equipment is strategically located.

Design 31342
1,560 Sq. Ft.; 13,256 Cu. Ft.

● Here is a relatively low-cost home with a majority of the features found in today's high priced homes. The three-bedroom sleeping area highlights two full baths. The living area is a huge room of approximately 25 feet in depth zoned for both formal living and dining activities. The kitchen is extremely well-planned and includes a built-in desk and pantry. The family room has a snack bar and sliding glass doors to the terrace. Blueprints include optional basement details.

Design 31357
1,258 Sq. Ft.; 13,606 Cu. Ft.

Design 31065
1,492 Sq. Ft.; 24,407 Cu. Ft.

● Here is a refreshing design that reflects all that is so appealing in good up-to-date exterior detailing and practical, efficient floor planning. The low pitched, wide overhanging roof, the glass gabled end with exposed rafters, the raised planter and the extended wing walls are all delightful exterior features. Of particular interest, is the formation of the front entrance court and side terrace resulting from the extension of the front living room wall. Inside, there is much to excite the new occupants. The quietly, formal living room will have plenty of light. The strategically located kitchen is ideal to view approaching callers. Master bedroom with bath, vanity and dressing room housing two closets will be welcomed by the parents.

Design 32703
1,445 Sq. Ft.; 30,300 Cu. Ft.

● This modified, hip-roofed contemporary design will be the answer for those who want something both practical, yet different, inside and out. The covered front walk sets the stage for entering a modest sized home with tremendous livability. The focal point will be the pleasant conversation lounge. It is sunken, partically open to the other living areas and shares the enjoyment of the thru-fireplace with the living room. There are two bedrooms, two full baths and a study. The kitchen is outstanding.

Design 32753
1,539 Sq. Ft.; 31,910 Cu. Ft.

● In this day and age of expensive building sites, projecting the attached garage from the front line of the house makes a lot of economic sense. It also lends itself to interesting roof lines and plan configurations. Here, a pleasing covered walkway to the front door results. A privacy wall adds an extra measure of design appeal and provides a sheltered terrace for the study/bedroom. You'll seldom find more livability in 1,539 square feet. Imagine, three bedrooms, two baths, a spacious living/dining area and a family room.

Design 32744
1,381 Sq. Ft.; 17,530 Cu. Ft.

● Here is a practical and an attractive contemporary home for that narrow building site. It is designed for efficiency with the small family or retired couple in mind. Sloping ceilings foster an extra measure of spaciousness. In addition to the master bedroom, there is the study that can also serve as the second bedroom or as an occasional guest room. The single bath is compartmented and its dual access allows it to serve living and sleeping areas more than adequately. Note raised hearth fireplace, snack bar, U-shaped kitchen, laundry, two terraces, etc.

Design 32106
1,520 Sq. Ft.; 30,658 Cu. Ft.

● Take a serious look at this highly integrated plan. It has a simple, straightforward, up-to-date exterior which will be pleasing on any site, whether out in the country or on a city block. The interior design will be just as pleasing and serve the family admirably for many years. Three bedrooms, one-and-a-half baths, formal and informal living areas plus a basement for additional space are just a portion of the delightful qualities that this home has to offer.

Design 31254
1,588 Sq. Ft.; 24,181 Cu. Ft.

● This is a great home for a relatively narrow building site. Measuring only 48 feet in width, this home could be located on almost any lot. The L-shaped configuration conveniently provides an area for a pool or an exceptionally large terrace or garden. In either case it will be a great place to enjoy the outdoors. The indoors will be enjoyed in the many conveniently located rooms including both formal and informal areas.

Design 32182 *1,558 Sq. Ft.; 280 Sq. Ft. - Atrium; 18,606 Cu. Ft.*

● What a great new dimension in living is represented by this unique contemporary design! Each of the major zones comprise a separate unit which, along with the garage, clusters around the atrium. High sloped ceilings and plenty of glass areas assure a feeling of spaciousness. The quiet living room will enjoy its privacy, while activities in the informal family room will be great fun functioning with the kitchen. A snack bar opens the kitchen to the atrium. The view, above right, shows portions of snack bar and the front entry looking through the glass wall. There are two full baths strategically located to service all areas conveniently. Storage facilities are excellent, indeed. Don't miss the storage potential found in the garage. There is a work bench and storage balcony above.

Design 31033
1,500 Sq. Ft.; 15,375 Cu. Ft.

OPTIONAL BASEMENT

● A unique plan with each of the three bedrooms, plus two full baths, located in the front. This results in the living areas and the kitchen overlooking and functioning with the rear terrace. The master bedroom has its own bath and fine closet facilities. The living room has excellent furniture placement possibilities. A fine feature. Optional basement details are included with the plan.

Design 33163
1,552 Sq. Ft.; 16,171 Cu. Ft.

OPTIONAL BASEMENT

● Four bedrooms and two full baths will very adequately serve the growing family occupying this appealing contemporary. Its perfectly rectangular shape means economical construction. Note the attractive built-in planter adjacent to the front door. The large storage area behind the carport will solve any storage problems. Laundry and wash room are strategically located to serve the family.

Design 31021
1,432 Sq. Ft.; 14,549 Cu. Ft.

OPTIONAL BASEMENT PLAN

● Behind the double front doors of this straight-forward, contemporary design there is a heap of living to be enjoyed. The large living room with its dramatic glass wall and attractive fireplace will never fail to elicit comments of delight. The master bedroom has a whole wall of wardrobe closets and a private bath. Another two bedrooms and a bath easily serve the family.

Design 31000
1,488 Sq. Ft.; 13,392 Cu. Ft.

OPTIONAL BASEMENT PLAN

● Living in this flat-roofed contemporary will be lots of fun. And little wonder when you consider the two large living areas, the outstanding kitchen, the zoning of the sleeping area, the outdoor terraces and the spacious front entrance court. Also included in this plan are two full baths, an attractive fireplace and a big carport.

Design 32821
1,363 Sq. Ft. - First Floor
351 Sq. Ft. - Second Floor
37,145 Cu. Ft.

**Mansard Roof
Adaptation**

A Trend House . . .

● Here is a truly unique house whose interior was designed with the current decade's economies, life-styles and demographics in mind. While functioning as a one-story home, the second floor provides an extra measure of livability when required. In addition, this two-story section adds to the dramatic appeal of both the exterior and the interior. Within only 1,363 square feet, this contemporary delivers refreshing and outstanding living patterns for those who are buying their first home, those who have raised their family and are looking for a smaller home and those in search of a retirement home. The center entrance routes traffic effectively to each area. The great room with its raised hearth fireplace, two-story arching and delightful glass areas is most distinctive. The kitchen is efficient and but a step from the dining room. The covered porch will provide an ideal spot for warm-weather, outdoor dining. The separate laundry room is strategically located. The sleeping area may consist of one bedroom and a study, or two bedrooms. Each room functions with the sheltered wood deck - a perfect location for a hot tub.

Design 32822
1,363 Sq. Ft. - First Floor
351 Sq. Ft. - Second Floor
36,704 Cu. Ft.

**Gable Roof
Version**

UPPER GREAT RM.

RAILING

CL.

LOUNGE / HOBBIES
16⁰ x 9²

SKYLITE

CL.

DN

RAILING

UPPER
FOYER

STOR. /
BATH

RAILING

BALCONY

LOUNGE / GUEST RM. /
GRANDCHILDREN'S RM.
16⁰ x 19²

CL.

RAILING

CL.

DN

RAILING

UPPER
FOYER

BATH

RAILING

ALTERNATE SECOND FLOOR

● The full bath is planned to have easy access to the master bedroom and living areas. Note the stall shower, tub, seat and vanity. The second floor offers two optional layouts. It may serve as a lounge, studio or hobby area overlooking the great room. Or, it may be built to function as a complete private guest room. It would be a great place for the visiting grandchildren. Don't miss the outdoor balcony. Additional livability and storage facilities may be developed in the basement. Then, of course, there are two exteriors to choose from. Design 32821, with its horizontal frame siding and deep, attractive cornice detail, is an eye-catcher. For those with a preference for a contemporary fashioned gable roof and vertical siding, there is Design 32822. With the living areas facing the south, these designs will enjoy benefits of passive solar exposure. The overhanging roofs will help provide relief from the high summer sun. This is surely a modest-sized floor plan which will deliver new dimensions in small-family livability.

...For the 80's and Decades to Come

Design 33207
1,460 Sq. Ft.; 25,068 Cu. Ft.

● Four bedrooms to satisfy the sleeping requirements of the large or growing family. In addition, there are two full baths nearby. They have a common plumbing wall to enable the installation of these two baths to represent a worthwhile savings. The bath for the master bedroom is also handy to the other three bedrooms. It has a built-in vanity. The main bath is strategically located only a few steps from the kitchen as well as the living area. The kitchen is conveniently located near the front door with the kitchen window overseeing the front yard. The living/dining room will enjoy the fireplace wall. Along with the living/dining room, the family room has sloped ceiling and access to the covered terrace.

Design 31943 *1,565 Sq. Ft.; 17,985 Cu. Ft.*

● This home will be a great investment. It starts right out representing economy because it will not require a wide expensive building site. The projecting two-car garage in no way affects the modest, overall, 50 foot width of the house. The favorable economics go even further. In less than 1,600 square feet there is a long list of convenient living features. They begin, of course, with the four sizable bedrooms. Two full baths with back-to-back plumbing will adequately serve the large family. A spacious living room overlooks the rear terrace and has a glass grille room divider. It also features fine wall space for flexible furniture placement. The informal, all-purpose family room functions with the kitchen and terrace.

Design 31057
1,320 Sq. Ft.; 13,741 Cu. Ft.

● Here is a relatively small contemporary with 1,320 square feet that is just loaded with livability. Its overall dimension of 56 feet means that it won't require a big, expensive piece of property either. The flexibility of the floor planning is great, too. Notice the room locations. The three bedrooms and compartmented bath occupy the far end of the house. The living room is by itself and will have privacy. The dining room is next to the kitchen and enjoys a view of the front court area. The family room functions ideally with the kitchen and the rear terrace. Other features include the wash room, the sloped ceilings, the snack bar, the attached garage, sliding glass doors and an abundance of closets.

Design 33203
1,291 Sq. Ft.; 23,625 Cu. Ft.

● The degree to which your family's living patterns will be efficient will depend upon the soundness of the basic floor plan. Here is an exceptionally practical arrangment for a medium sized home. Traffic patterns will be most flexible. The work area is strategically located close to the front door and it will function ideally with both the indoor and outdoor informal living areas. The master bath will serve the living room and the sleeping area. The second bath will serve the work area, the family room and third bedroom. Note stall shower.

Design 33212
1,493 Sq. Ft.; 16,074 Cu. Ft.

● Imagine ushering your first visitors through the front door of your new home. After you have placed their coats in the big closet in the front entry, you will show them your three sizable bedrooms and the two full baths. Next, you will take them through the separate dining area, the efficient kitchen and into the large family room with its wall of built-in storage units. Your visitors will comment about the sliding glass doors which open onto the terrace from the family room.

Design 31072
1,232 Sq. Ft.; 22,484 Cu. Ft.

● Low-pitched overhanging roof, vertical siding and patterned masonry screen wall create a charming exterior for this house. A fireplace divides the living room from the entry hall. Seven-foot high cabinets separate the kitchen from the living/dining area. The dining area opens through sliding glass doors to a private covered porch and the rear terrace. The informal area is enhanced by a wall of windows overlooking the terrace and a three-foot high built-in planter. For recreation and bulk storage there is a full basement.

Design 32892
1,623 Sq. Ft.; 38,670 Cu. Ft.

● What a striking contemporary! It houses an efficient floor plan with many outstanding features. The foyer has a sloped ceiling and an open staircase to the basement. To the right of the foyer is the work center. Note the snack bar, laundry and covered dining porch, along with the step-saving kitchen. Both the gathering and dining rooms overlook the backyard. Each of the three bedrooms has access to an outdoor area. Now, just think of the potential use of the second floor loft. Its 160 square feet of livability could be used as a den, sewing room, lounge or any of many other activities. It overlooks the gathering room and front foyer and has two large skylights.

Design 32809
1,551 Sq. Ft.; 42,615 Cu. Ft.

● One-story living can be very rewarding and this contemporary home will be just that. Study the indoor-outdoor living relationships which are offered in the back of the plan. Sliding glass doors are in each of the rear rooms leading to the terrace. The formal dining room has a second set of doors to the porch. Many enjoyable hours will be spent here in the hot tub. A sloped ceiling with skylights is above the hot tub area. Back to the interior, there is a large gathering room. It, too, has a sloped ceiling which will add to its spacious appearance. The interior kitchen is conveniently located between the formal and informal dining areas. Two, or optional three, bedrooms are ready to serve the small family.

Design 32864
1,387 Sq. Ft.; 29,160 Cu. Ft.

● Projecting the garage to the front of a house is very economical in two ways. One, it reduces the required lot size for building (in this case the overall width is under 50 feet). And, two, it will protect the interior from street noise and unfavorable winds. Many other characteristics about this design deserve mention, too. The entrance court and covered porch are a delightful way to enter this home. Upon entering, the foyer will take you to the various areas. The interior kitchen has an adjacent breakfast room and a snack bar on the gathering room side. Here, one will enjoy a sloped ceiling and a fireplace. A study with a wet bar is adjacent. If need be, adjust the plan and make the study the third bedroom. Sliding glass doors in the study and master bedroom open to the terrace.

Design 32591 1,428 Sq. Ft.; 21,725 Cu. Ft.

63'-8"

TERRACE

TERRACE

LIVING RM.
13⁰ x 18⁸

DINING RM.
10⁴ x 9⁰

BED RM.
10⁰ x 11⁶

BED RM.
10⁰ x 11⁶

CL

KITCHEN
10⁰ x 9⁰

MASTER
BED RM
11⁰ x 16⁰

REF'G RANGE B.C.

S

D.W.

CL

48'-8"

HALL

LINEN

ENTRY

NOOK
7⁸ x 7²

DRESSING   BATH

BATH

DN.

PANTRY

CL

CL

CL

PORCH

CURB

COVERED WALK

GARAGE
21⁴ x 21⁴

● A flowing terrace! The point of unity between interior and exterior in this distinctive home. This unusual terrace is accessible from every room except the kitchen . . . but designed to provide privacy as well. Inside, the spacious living and dining rooms feature two sets of sliding glass doors onto the terrace . . . allowing parties to spill outside during warm weather. And offering a scenic view all year round. Three bedrooms, all with sliding doors onto the terrace. Including a master suite with a dressing room and private bath. Plus its own secluded section of the terrace . . . perfect for solitary sunbathing or romantic nightcaps. Good times and easy work! There's an efficient kitchen with lots of work space and a large storage pantry. Plus a separate breakfast nook to make casual meals convenient and pleasant. This home creates its own peaceful enviroment! It's especially pleasing to people who love the outdoors.

CONTEMPORARY DESIGNS 1600-2000 Sq. Ft. . . . *as high-*

lighted in this section will appeal to those with an expanded building budget. In many cases they will require a larger building site than their smaller counterparts. While specific designs in this section may not be more expensive to build, or deliver more livability, than some designs in the prior section, the larger of the homes here are on the upscale side. When studying these houses, don't miss their distinctive exterior design impact. As you review the interiors list the features that will make a contribution to the improvement of your family's living patterns and, hence, enjoyment. What are everybody's favorite highlights?

Design 32702
1,636 Sq. Ft.; 38,700 Cu. Ft.

● A rear living room with a sloping ceiling, built-in book-cases, a raised hearth fireplace and sliding glass doors to the rear living terrace highlight this design. If desired, bi-fold doors permit this room to function with the adjacent study. An open railing next to the stairs to the basement recreation area fosters additional spaciousness. The kitchen has plenty of cabinet and cupboard space. It features informal eating space and is but a step or two from the separate dining room. Note side dining terrace. Each of the three rooms in the sleeping wing has direct access to outdoor living. The master bedroom highlights a huge walk-in wardrobe closet, dressing room with built-in vanity and private bath with large towel storage closet. Projecting the two-car garage with its twin doors to the front not only contributes to an interesting exterior, but reduces the size of the building site required for this home.

Design 32792
1,944 Sq. Ft.; 37,505 Cu. Ft.

● Indoor-outdoor living hardly could be improved upon in this contemporary design. All of the rear rooms have sliding glass doors to the large terrace. Divide the terrace in three parts and the nook and dining room have access to a dining terrace, the gathering room to a living terrace and two bedrooms to a lounging terrace. A delightful way to bring the outdoors view inside. Other fine features include the efficient kitchen which has plenty of storage space and an island range, a first floor laundry with stairs to the basement and a powder room adjacent to the front door.

Design 32797
1,791 Sq. Ft.; 37,805 Cu. Ft.

● The exterior appeal of this delightful one-story is sure to catch the attention of all who pass by. The overhanging roof adds an extra measure of shading along with the privacy wall which shelters the front court and entry. The floor plan also will be outstanding to include both leisure and formal activities. The gathering room has a sloped ceiling, sliding glass door to rear terrace and a thru-fireplace to the family room. This room also has access to the terrace and it includes the informal eating area. A pass-thru from the U-shaped kitchen to the eating area makes serving a breeze. Formal dining can be done in the front dining room. The laundry area is adjacent to the kitchen and garage and houses a washroom. Peace and quiet can be achieved in the study. The sleeping zone consists of three bedrooms and two full back-to-back baths. Additional space will be found in the basement.

Design 32790
2,075 Sq. Ft.; 45,630 Cu. Ft.

● Enter this contemporary home through the
double front doors and immediately view the
sloped ceiling in the living room. This room
will be a sheer delight when it comes to formal
entertaining. It has easy access to the kitchen
and also a powder room is nearby. The work
area will be convenient. An island work center
with snack bar is in the kitchen. The laundry is
adjacent to the service entrance and stairs leading to the basement. This area is planned to be
a real "step saver". The sleeping wing consists
of two family bedrooms, bath and master bedroom suite. Maybe the most attractive feature of
this design is the rear, covered porch with skylights above. It is accessible by way of sliding
glass doors in the family/dining area, living
room and master bedroom. This design will
prove to be efficient and livable.

Design 32330
1,854 Sq. Ft.; 30,001 Cu. Ft.

● Your family will never tire of the living patterns offered by this appealing home with its low-pitched, wide overhanging roof. The masonry masses of the exterior are pleasing. While the blueprints call for the use of stone, you may wish to substitute brick veneer. Sloping ceiling and plenty of glass will assure the living area of a fine feeling of spaciousness. The covered porches enhance the enjoyment of outdoor living. Two baths serve the three bedroom sleeping area.

Design 33165
1,940 Sq. Ft.; 20,424 Cu. Ft.

● A practical plan with a contemporary facade. The center entrance encourages fine traffic circulation. To the right of the entry hall is the formal living area with its sunken living room and separate dining room separated by an attractive built-in planter. To the left of the entry hall is the three bedroom, two full bath sleeping zone. At the end of the entrance hall is the informal living area featuring the family room, efficient kitchen and laundry room.

Floor Plan Labels

64'-0"

52'-5"

MASTER BED RM.
19⁴ x 12⁴

WALK-IN CL.

BED RM.
9⁰ x 9⁸

BATH

TERRACE

BATH

BED RM.
9⁰ x 9⁸

FAMILY RM.
15⁰ x 13⁴

NOOK
9⁰ x 6⁸

LNDRY.

STORAGE

AIR COND.

SLOPED CEILING

SNACK BAR

KIT.
8⁸ x 9⁸

REF. RANGE OVEN

SKYLIGHT

SLOPED CEILING

BED RM.
12⁸ x 9⁸

FOYER

SLOPED CEILING

RAILING

LIVING RM.
15⁰ x 13⁴

DINING
9⁰ x 11⁰

PORCH

CARPORT
19⁸ x 21⁸

Design 32312
1,703 Sq. Ft.; 18,801 Cu. Ft.

● If you like contemporary living patterns to go with your refreshingly distinctive exterior, this four bedroom design may be the perfect choice for you and your family. Essentially of frame construction with vertical siding, brick veneer is used prudently to foster an appealing contrast in exterior materials. The covered front entrance leads to the centered foyer which effectively routes traffic to the well-zoned interior. The living and dining rooms function together for formal entertaining. The family room, nook and kitchen also function well together. This informal living zone is readily accessible to the rear terrace.

Design 31917

1,728 Sq. Ft.; 32,486 Cu. Ft.

● Imagine your family living in this appealing one-story home. Think of how your living habits will adjust to the delightful patterns offered here. Flexibility is the byword; for there are two living areas — the front, formal living room and the rear, informal family room. There are two dining areas — the dining room overlooking the front yard and the breakfast room looking out upon the rear yard. There are outstanding bath facilities — a full bath for the master bedroom and one that will be handy to the living areas as a powder room. Then there is the extra wash room just where you need it — handy to the kitchen, the basement and the outdoors.

Design 31891

1,986 Sq. Ft.; 23,022 Cu. Ft.

● There is much more to a house than just its exterior. And while the appeal of this home would be difficult to beat, it is the living potential of the interior that gives this design such a high ranking. The sunken living room with its adjacent dining room is highlighted by the attractive fireplace, the raised planter and the distinctive glass panels. A raised hearth fireplace, snack bar and sliding glass doors which open to the outdoor deck are features of the family room. The work center area is efficient. It has plenty of storage space and a laundry area.

Design 31396

1,664 Sq. Ft.; 30,229 Cu. Ft.

● Three bedrooms, 2½ baths, a formal dining area, a fine family room and an attached two-car garage are among the highlights of this frame home. The living-dining area is delightfully spacious with the fireplace wall, having book shelves at each end, functioning as a practical area divider. The many storage units found in this home will be a topic of conversion. The cabinets above the strategically located washer and dryer, the family room storage wall and walk-in closet and the garage facilities are particularly noteworthy. Blueprints show how to build this house with and without a basement.

Design 31798
1,720 Sq. Ft.; 17,280 Cu. Ft.

● Has your family ever wished they lived in a house where there could be a complete separation of the parents' and the children's living and sleeping facilities? If so, consider this L-shaped house. You will note here that such a separation does not neccessitate any huge or palatial-size floor plan. Clever planning has resulted in this fine, modest-size plan. Try to visualize how your family will function in this house. The two full baths service their respective areas well. The family room will be the teenagers' informal activities area. Sloping ceilings enhance the spaciousness of the interior. Free-standing built-in cabinet work is open above 7½ feet and carries over the doorways in the form of a valance. This is just one of the many features which will attract you to this fine design.

Design 31785 *1,868 Sq. Ft.; 22,589 Cu. Ft.*

● A refreshing exterior which will be like a breath of fresh air to your new neighborhood. This exquisite facade is reminiscent of Japanese architecture. Among the exterior features is the *Irimoya* roof, a combination of gable and hip styles. The wide eaves, *sori*, protect against the rain and the high, hot sun of summer, yet let in the low winter sunlight. The lattice-work grilles at the front resemble the *shoji* screens that the Japanese use on the exteriors of their homes. A study of the floor plan reveals a fine awareness of the outdoors. The interior features both formal and informal living areas. Kitchen eating space, plus a formal dining room is provided. There are plenty of bath and storage facilities.

TERRACE

8'-5"   76'-5"

TERRACE

FAMILY RM.
18⁰ x 16⁰

LIVING
21⁰ x 16⁰

BED RM.
11⁸ x 12⁰

BED RM.
11⁸ x 12⁰

PORCH

SLOPE CEIL'G   RAISED HEARTH   SLOPE CEIL'G   SLOPE CEIL'G   SLOPE CEIL'G

MASTER
BED RM.
11⁸ x 15⁴

SLOPE CEIL'G

CHEST   CHEST

CL.   CL.   LIN.   LIN.   CL.   CL.

SNACK BAR

RANGE   AIR COND.   STOR.

SLOPE CEIL'G

ENTRY HALL

CL.

STOR.

BATH   BATH

CL.

KIT.
12⁰ x 11⁰

REF'G

DINING
13⁴ x 11⁰

PORCH

56'-5"

MUD ROOM

CL.   D.   W.   W.R.

26'-9"

GARAGE
23⁴ x 21⁴

SNACK BAR

RANGE   STOR.   BSM'S

KIT.
12⁰ x 11⁰

DN.

REF'G   DN.

MUD RM.

CL.   D.   W.   W.R.

OPTIONAL BASEMENT

Design 31019
1,996 Sq. Ft.; 20,550 Cu. Ft.

● Here is an attention-getter wherever you build it—in town, or on the outskirts of town. The curving drive approach has a way of establishing an impressive setting. The roofs are pitched low and they overhang to create that low-slung effect. The window treatment is simple, yet appealing, while the natural stone masses and the planting enhance the visual impact. The double front doors are recessed to provide shelter during inclement weather. The kitchen-family room area looks out upon its own side terrace, while the formal living room and bedrooms have their rear terrace.

Floor plan labels:

BED RM. 13⁰ x 11⁰

FAMILY RM. 20⁰ x 13⁰

CL.

CL.

STOR.

MASTER BED RM. 17⁰ x 13⁰

CL.

CL.

STOR.

TERRACE

LIN.

BATH

BATH

LINEN

DINING RM. 9⁸ x 10⁸

KITCHEN 10 x 8

D.W. S.

REF'G RANGE OVENS

AIR COND.

WASH DRY

PN'TRY

UTILITY RM. 17⁰ x 7⁰

CL.

SCREEN

DN.

RAIL

ENTRY

DN.

BED RM. 11⁰ x 13⁰

LIVING RM. 18⁰ x 13⁰

CL.

CL.

PORCH

GARAGE 19⁴ x 21⁴

56'-10"

48'-10"

Design 32351   1,862 Sq. Ft.; 22,200 Cu. Ft.

● The extension of the wide over-hanging roof of this distinctive home provides shelter for the walkway to the front door. A raised brick planter adds appeal to the outstanding exterior design. The living patterns offered by this plan are delightfully different, yet ex-tremely practical. Notice the separation of the master bedroom from the other two bedrooms. While assuring an extra measure of quiet privacy for the parents, this master bedroom location may be ideal for a live-in-relative. Locating the kitchen in the middle of the plan frees up valuable outside wall space and leads to interesting planning. The front living room is sunken for dramatic appeal and need not have any cross-room traffic. The utility room houses the laundry and the heating and cooling equipment.

Design 32363 1,978 Sq. Ft.; 27,150 Cu. Ft.

● You will have a lot of fun deciding what you like best about this home with its eye-catching glass-gabled living room and wrap-around raised planter. A covered porch shelters the double front doors. Projecting to the rear is a family room identical in size with the formal living room. Between these two rooms there are features galore. There is the efficient kitchen with pass-thru and informal eating space. Then, there is the laundry with a closet, pantry and the basement stairs nearby. Also, a full bath featuring a stall shower. The dining room has a sloped ceiling and an appealing, open vertical divider which acts as screening from the entry. The three bedroom, two bath sleeping zone is sunken. The raised hearth fireplace in the living room has an adjacent wood box.

Design 32795
1,952 Sq. Ft.; 43,500 Cu. Ft.

● This three-bedroom design leaves no room for improvement. Any size family will find it difficult to surpass the fine qualities that this home offers. Begin with the exterior. This fine contemporary design has open trellis work above the front, covered private court. This area is sheltered by a privacy wall extending from the projecting garage. Inside, the floor plan will be just as breathtaking. Begin at the foyer and choose a direction. To the right is the sleeping wing equipped with three bedrooms and two baths. Straight ahead from the foyer is the gathering room with thru-fireplace to the dining room. To the right is the work center. This area includes a breakfast room, a U-shaped kitchen and laundry.

Design 32754
1,844 Sq. Ft.; 26,615 Cu. Ft.

● This really is a most dramatic and refreshing contemporary home. The slope of its wide overhanging roofs is carried right indoors to provide an extra measure of spaciousness. The U-shaped privacy wall of the front entrance area provides an appealing outdoor living spot accessible from the front bedroom. The rectangular floor plan will be economical to build. Notice the efficient use of space and how it all makes its contribution to outstanding livability. The small family will find its living patterns delightful, indeed. Two bedrooms and two full baths comprise the sleeping zone. The open planning of the L-shaped living and dining rooms is most desirable. The thru-fireplace is just a great room divider. The kitchen and breakfast nook function well together. There is laundry and mechanical room nearby.

Design 32796
1,828 Sq. Ft.; 39,990 Cu. Ft.

● This home features a front living room with sloped ceiling and sliding glass doors which lead to a front private court. What a delightful way to introduce this design. This bi-nuclear design has a great deal to offer. First - the children's and parent's sleeping quarters are on opposite ends of this house to assure the utmost in privacy. Each area has its own full bath. The interior kitchen is a great idea. It frees up valuable wall space for the living areas exclusive use. There is a snack bar in the kitchen/family room for those very informal meals. Also, a planning desk is in the family room. The dining room is conveniently located near the kitchen plus it has a built-in china cabinet. The laundry area has plenty of storage closets plus the stairs to the basement. This home will surely be a welcome addition to any setting.

Design 32902
1,632 Sq. Ft. - First Floor; 37,427 Cu. Ft.

● A sun space highlights this passive solar design. It has access from the kitchen, dining room and garage. It will be a great place to enjoy meals because of its location. Three skylights highlight the interior - one in the kitchen, laundry and master bath. An air-locked vestibule helps this design's energy efficiency. Interior livability is excellent. The living/-dining room has a sloping ceiling, fireplace and two sets of sliding glass doors to the terrace. This area will cater to numerous family activities. Additional activities can take place in the basement. Note its open staircase. Three bedrooms are in the sleeping wing. The square and cubic footages of the sun space are 216 and 1,944 respectively and are not included in the above figures.

GREENHOUSE 22⁶ x 10⁴

TERRACE

TERRACE

69'-8"

GATHERING RM. 24⁰ x 15⁰-17⁴

STUDY/ BEDROOM 11⁰ x 13⁴

GREENHOUSE 12⁸ x 9⁴

BATH

HOT TUB

BRKFST. RM. 10⁸ x 9⁰

DINING AREA

THRU-FIREPLACE

SLOPED CEILING

57'-0"

KITCHEN 10⁸ x 10⁸

CLERESTORY ABOVE

FOYER

BATH

BEDROOM 11⁸ x 10⁰ + BAY

MASTER BEDROOM 13⁰ x 14⁸

COVERED PORCH

GARAGE 21⁴ x 21²

Design 32886

1,733 Sq. Ft.; 34,986 Cu. Ft.

● This one-story house is attractive with its contemporary exterior. It has many excellent features to keep you and your family happy for many years. For example, notice the spacious gathering room with sliding glass doors that allow easy access to the greenhouse. Another exciting feature of this room is that you will receive an abundance of sunshine through the clerestory windows. Also, this plan offers you two nice-sized bedrooms. The master suite is not only roomy but also unique because through both the bedroom and the bath you can enter a greenhouse with a hot tub. The hot tub will be greatly appreciated after a long, hard day at work. Don't forget to note the breakfast room with access to the terrace. You will enjoy the efficient kitchen that will make preparing meals a breeze. A greenhouse window here is charming. An appealing, open staircase leads to the basement. The square and cubic footages of the greenhouses are 394 and 4,070 respectively and are not included in the above figures.

Design 33139
1,680 Sq. Ft.; 17,808 Cu. Ft.

● Whatever the setting - in the mountains or on the flat lands - this contemporary will be an attractive addition. While this house guards its privacy from the street, it promotes wonderful indoor-outdoor relationship to the rear. A study of the plan reveals five sliding glass doors. In addition to the functional rear terrace areas, there is the court and side terrace each of which will enjoy seclusion resulting from the patterned masonry walls. The interior is extremely interesting and practical. Notice the separation of the children's and parents' bedrooms. A full bath serves each. The centrally located U-shaped kitchen is adjacent to the breakfast eating area, the snack bar and the family dining room.

Design 32201
1,811 Sq. Ft.; 32,708 Cu. Ft.

● This appealing L-shaped contemporary with its interesting glass areas, raised planter and prudent use of contrasting exterior materials has much to offer the modest sized family. Its fine zoning will lead to pleasurable living patterns. Notice the sleeping wing. There are two sizable bedrooms, plus a smaller bedroom which may instead be a study, sewing room or a guest room. There are two baths and positively extraordinary storage facilities. The living zone has a big living room and a family dining room. Sloping beamed ceilings highlight these rooms. The homemaker's kitchen will be a joy in which to function. A pass-thru leads to the snack bar.

Design 31153 *1,616 Sq. Ft.; 16,256 Cu. Ft.*

● The simple appeal of this contemporary design is to be found in the solid brick masses, the delicate patterned grille work and the low-pitched roof. Inside the iron gate is the pleasing flower court. The projecting carport or garage, if you wish, offers the possibility of the development of an impressive drive court approach. Inside, the plan is certainly unique.

The room relationships are excellent and the traffic patterns are orderly. You will love the indoor-outdoor accessibility. Blueprints for this particular design include details for both basement and non-basement construction. Don't miss the sloped ceilings, 2½ baths and all those closets.

Design 31129
1,904 Sq. Ft.; 34,066 Cu. Ft.

● Study this floor plan with care, for there is much to recommend it to the large family. The living room and separate dining area look out upon the rear yard. Sliding glass doors permit the dining area to function with the terrace — a delightful indoor-outdoor living feature. An appealing two-way fireplace may be enjoyed from both the living and dining areas. The efficient U-shaped kitchen overlooks the front yard and is but a few steps from the entry hall as well as the service entrance and garage.

Design 33219
1,960 Sq. Ft.; 31,643 Cu. Ft.

● Here is a delightfully tailored contemporary with a low-pitched roof and a wide overhang. Its window treatment is simple and the brick masses are pleasing. The raised planters add that little extra touch thus making a pretty picture truly delightful. It would be difficult to predict which would be the favored spot — sitting before the fireplace in the living room, or the family room. Two full baths serve the three bedroom sleeping area, while an extra wash room is adjacent to the mud room.

Design 31036
1,912 Sq. Ft.; 18,785 Cu. Ft.

● This pleasing contemporary design represents a fine combination of great exterior appeal and wonderful interior planning. The exterior is completely frame and features delightful glass areas protected by the wide overhanging roof. Although not a part of the house itself, the long planter adds notably to the overall appeal. The double doors of the center entry will be an attractive feature of the exterior. The flow of traffic throughout the plan will be very flexible and convenient.

Design 31867

1,692 Sq. Ft. — Excluding Atrium; 21,383 Cu. Ft.

● Looking for a new house involves a number of varied considerations. One that is most basic involves what you would like your family's living patterns to be. If you would like to introduce your family to something that is different and is sure to be fun for all, consider this dramatic atrium house. Parents and children alike will be thrilled by the experience and the enviroment engendered by this outdoor living area indoors. A skylight provides for the protection during inclement weather without restricting the flood of natural light. Notice how this atrium functions with the various areas. Observe relationships between children's rooms and family room; master bedroom and living room.

Design 31283

1,904 Sq. Ft. – Excluding Atrium; 18,659 Cu. Ft.

● Here is a unique home whose livable area is basically a perfect square. Completely adaptable to a narrow building site, the presence of the atrium permits the enjoyment of private outdoor living "indoors". Sliding glass doors open onto this delightful atrium with its attractive planting areas.

Design 32383

1,984 Sq. Ft. – Excluding Atrium; 20,470 Cu. Ft.

● Design your home around an atrium and you will enjoy living patterns unlike any you have experienced in the past. This interior area is assured complete outdoor privacy. Five sets of sliding glass doors enhance the accessibility of this unique area. With the two-car garage projecting from the front of the house, this design will not require a large piece of property. Worthy of particular note is the separation of the master bedroom from the other three bedrooms - a fine feature to assure peace and quiet. Side-by-side are the formal and informal living rooms. Both function with the rear terrace. Separating the two rooms is the thru-fireplace and double access wood box.

Design 31237
1,616 Sq. Ft.; 15,150 Cu. Ft.

● The distinctiveness of contemporary design takes many forms. Here the trim flat roofs set the character aided by the vertical siding, the wood posts and the masses of glass. The front entranceway is covered and is enhanced by the picturesque court. The plan is equally unique since it features the two children's bedrooms functioning with the family room and the parents' master bedroom functioning with the formal living room. Functional terraces play their part: the play terrace is adjacent to the children's area; the quiet terrace is next to the parents' room and the living terrace services the dining and living rooms.

Design 31932
1,678 Sq. Ft.; 17,115 Cu. Ft.

● Here is a unique contemporary design whose projecting wings reach out to enclose a spacious, front court. The high privacy wall helps support the covering for the walkway inside. This enchanting area will be enjoyed the year-round. Windows in the living room permit a fine view of this area and the undisturbed beauty of its landscaping, whatever the season. A study of the basic, L-shaped floor plan reveals convenient living patterns. The informal family room and the formal living/dining area feature sloping ceilings for a feeling of spaciousness. Study the plan's other areas.

Design 32234
1,857 Sq. Ft.; 22,748 Cu. Ft.

● Planned to assure privacy from the street, this contemporary home sacrifices nothing in the way of natural light. Plenty of sliding glass doors and plastic skylights provide an abundance of daytime light. The zoning is interesting and practical. To one side is the sleeping zone; to the other, the living zone. The master bedroom features a huge walk-in closet and private bath. A handy corner of the family room will provide the space for family dining. The varied activities of the family can be pursued with plenty of space left over. Note storage wall. Two-way fireplace separates family and living rooms.

Design 31884
1,925 Sq. Ft.; 26,062 Cu. Ft.

● If you are searching for something with an air of distinction both inside and out then search no more. You could hardly improve upon what this home has to offer. You will forever be proud of the impressive hip-roof, angular facade. Its interest will give it an identity all its own. As for the interior, your everyday living patterns will be a delight, indeed. And little wonder, clever zoning and a fine feeling of spaciousness set the stage. As you stand in the entrance hall, you look across the tip of a four foot high planter into the sunken living room. Having an expanse of floor space, the wall of windows and the raised hearth fireplace, the view will be dramatic. Notice covered porch, play terrace and quiet terrace which will provide great outdoor enjoyment.

LOW BUDGET HOMES UNDER 1200 Sq. Ft. . . . *may*

serve any of three groups of home buyers. First, the entry-level family which is about to begin the planning of its first new home. Such families are often small ones and called upon to operate within the confines of a restricted building budget. Second, the empty-nester family which is comprised of a couple who has raised children and seen them leave the home. These families may now be looking for a smaller, less expensive home than that in which they raised their children. Third, the family in search of an efficient, conventionally designed second home. This may, or may not, be used as a vacation home. Surely fine livability at modest cost.

Design 32755
1,200 Sq. Ft.; 23,925 Cu. Ft.

● Here is truly an outstanding, low-cost design created to return all the pride of ownership and livability a small family or retired couple would ask of a new home. The living/dining area measures a spacious 23 feet. It has a fireplace and two sets of sliding glass doors leading to the large rear terrace. The two bedrooms also have access to this terrace. The kitchen is a real step-saver and has a pantry nearby. The study, which has sliding glass doors to the front porch, will function as that extra all-purpose room. Use it for sewing, guests, writing or reading or just plain napping. The basement offers the possibility for the development of additional recreation space. Note the storage area at the side of the garage. Many years of enjoyable living will surely be obtained in this home designed in the contemporary fashion.

Design 31297
1,034 Sq. Ft.; 11,324 Cu. Ft.

● The U-shape of this appealing home qualifies it for a narrow building site. The efficiency of the floor plan recommends it for convenient living during the retirement years. The charm of the exterior surely makes it a prize-winner. The attractive wood fence and its lamp post complete the enclosure of the flower court—a delightful setting for the walk to the covered front entrance. The work area is outstanding. There is the laundry with closet space, an extra wash room and a fine kitchen with eating space.

Design 31309
1,100 Sq. Ft.; 15,600 Cu. Ft.

● Here is a real low-cost charmer. Delightful proportion and an effective use of materials characterize this Colonial version. Vertical boards and battens, a touch of stone and pleasing window treatment catch the eye. The compact, economical plan offers spacious formal living and dining areas plus a family room. The kitchen is strategically located—it overlooks the rear yard and is but a few steps from the outdoor terrace. The attached garage has a large storage and utility area to the rear.

Design 31364
1,142 Sq. Ft.; 13,510 Cu. Ft.

● The family working within the confines of a restricted building budget will find this eye-catching traditional ranch home the solution to its housing needs. The brick exterior with its recessed front entrance, wood shutters, bowed window, attached garage and wood fence is charming, indeed. The living room is free of cross-room traffic and lends itself to effective and flexible furniture placement. The master bedroom has its own private bath with stall shower, while the main bath features a built-in vanity and adjacent linen storage.

Design 31300
1,008 Sq. Ft.; 19,313 Cu. Ft.

● The projecting garage with its bulk storage area adds a full measure of design distinction. Behind the garage is a family room which functions with the kitchen.

- 53'-4"
- 48'-0"
- 24'-0"
- 36'-0"
- TERRACE
- BED RM. 11⁸ x 11⁶
- BED RM. 9⁰ x 11⁶
- KIT. 8⁰ x 8⁰
- FAMILY RM. 15⁸ x 11⁴
- RANGE / REF'S
- BED RM. 10⁰ x 11⁶
- BATH
- LIVING RM. 17⁴ x 11⁶
- STORAGE
- GARAGE 11⁴ x 23⁸

Design 33221
976 Sq. Ft.; 9,523 Cu. Ft.

● This hip-roof home has a wide over-hang. The plan features excellent storage facilities. The kitchen-dining area is spacious and overlooks the rear yard. Note the optional carport with storage area.

Floor plan labels:
- 40'-0"
- 24'-5"
- 12'-0"
- 4'-0" / 8'-0"
- 26'-5"
- TERRACE
- TERRACE
- BED RM. 11⁴ x 10⁴
- STORAGE 6⁸ x 5⁰
- KITCHEN - DINING 15⁰ x 10⁴
- STORAGE 7⁴ x 5⁴
- STOR. 4⁰ x 5⁰
- BATH
- KITCHEN-DINING RM.
- RANGE / REF. G
- HTR
- BED RM. 11⁴ x 10⁴
- BED RM. 10⁸ x 10⁰
- LIVING RM. 14⁴ x 12⁸
- LIVING RM.
- CARPORT 12⁰ x 26⁵
- OPTIONAL CARPORT PLAN

Design 31301
1,056 Sq. Ft.; 19,536 Cu. Ft.

● Charming is just the word to describe this L-shaped traditional home. Note formal living and informal family rooms, U-shaped kitchen and extra wash room.

Design 33223
1,032 Sq. Ft.; 10,752 Cu. Ft.

● The master bedroom and kitchen of this efficient plan have direct access to the wash room. A full bath is convenient to all three bedrooms. The kitchen is but a few steps from the rear yard.

Design 32163 *864 Sq. Ft.; 16,554 Cu. Ft.*

● Traditional charm is an apt description of this low-cost one story. Every foot of space makes its vital contribution to total livability. There is a full basement.

● A hip-roofed contemporary with an attached carport. Both kitchen and dining room accessible to rear terrace. List the many storage units. Don't miss linen closets.

Design 32166 *864 Sq. Ft.; 8,448 Cu. Ft.*

● A compact, small home with its full measure of built-in efficiency. Inside bath frees valuable outside wall space for more effective planning. Three bedrooms.

Design 32164 864 Sq. Ft.; 9,245 Cu. Ft.

Design 32165
880 Sq. Ft.; 16,945 Cu. Ft.

● Whether called upon to function as a two or a three bedroom home, this attractive design will serve its occupants ideally for many years. There are two eating areas.

Design 32159 1,077 Sq. Ft.; 11,222 Cu. Ft.

● A perfect rectangle which will be easy and economical to build. There is an extra wash room, family kitchen, three bedrooms, full bath plus powder room and bulk storage area in the garage.

Design 33213
1,060 Sq. Ft.; 18,608 Cu. Ft.

● It would be difficult to find a design with more livability built into its 1,060 square feet. There are features galore. Make a list.

Design 31399
1,040 Sq. Ft.; 11,783 Cu. Ft.

● A real winner which will surely satisfy the restricted building budget, while returning a tremendous amount in the way of convenient living and pride of ownership.

Design 33222
1,128 Sq. Ft.; 12,192 Cu. Ft.

● A compact, four bedroom home for the growing family. A study of the floor plan reveals a most economical and efficient use of space.

Design 33224
960 Sq. Ft.; 17,453 Cu. Ft.

● This three bedroom frame home has a wide overhanging hip-roof and an attached carport with a storage unit. Family room-kitchen area is spacious.

Design 32153 960 Sq. Ft.; 18,432 Cu. Ft.

● If you can't make up your mind as to which of the delightful traditional exteriors you like best on the opposing page, you need not decide now. The blueprints you receive show details for the construction of all three front exteriors. However, before you order, decide whether you wish your next home to have a basement or not. If you prefer the basement plan order Design 32153 above. Should your preference be for a non-basement plan you should order blueprints for Design 32154 below. Whatever your choice, you'll forever love the charm of its exterior and the comfort and convenience of the interior. The three bedrooms will serve your family ideally.

Design 32154 960 Sq. Ft.; 10,675 Cu. Ft.

Design 32194
882 Sq. Ft.; 10,408 Cu. Ft.

● Here is a basic 36 x 24 foot rectangle that can be built with either the contemporary or traditional exterior. What's your preference? Observe the grouping of plumbing facilities. This is a positive economy factor. The kitchen is sizable and has plenty of space for eating. There will be no lack of space to put things with all the closet and storage areas. The living room has space for effective furniture placement. The washer and dryer are strategically situated at the source of most soiled linen. There is a recessed sliding door between the kitchen and the vestibule.

Design 32195

1,042 Sq. Ft.; 12,840 Cu. Ft. - Non-Basement
19,577 Cu. Ft. - Basement

NON BASEMENT PLAN

BASEMENT PLAN

● The construction blueprints you order for this design will feature a number of options. You will enjoy making your decisions on which is your favorite traditional exterior. Then, you and your family will also decide on whether you want to build a basement or non-basement house. Finally, you have the choice of whether or not to have a carport. Three bedrooms, bath, kitchen and living room are standard. Study the plan carefully.

Design 31311 *1,050 Sq. Ft.; 11,370 Cu. Ft.*

● Delightful design and effective, flexible planning comes in little packages, too. This fine traditional exterior with its covered front entrance features an alternate basement plan. Note how the non-basement layout provides a family room and mud room, while the basement option shows kitchen eating and dining room. Sensible planning.

OPTIONAL BASEMENT PLAN

Design 31531
936 Sq. Ft.; 12,252 Cu. Ft.

● This is but another example of delightful custom design applied to a small home. The detailing of the windows and the door, plus the effective use of siding and brick contribute to the charm. The attached garage helps make the house appear even bigger than it really is. The front-to-rear living/dining area opens onto the rear terrace through sliding glass doors. The washer and dryer with wall cabinets above complete the efficient work center area. Observe extra kitchen closet.

Design 31522
960 Sq. Ft.; 18,077 Cu. Ft.

● Certainly a home to make its occupants proud. The front exterior is all brick veneer, while the remainder of the house and garage is horizontal siding. The slightly overhanging roof, the wood shutters and the carriage lights flanking the front door are among the features that will surely catch the eyes of the passerby. The living room has excellent wall space for furniture placement. The family room, the full basement and the attached garage are other features. Don't miss the sliding glass doors.

56'-0"

TERRACE

MASTER
BED RM.
10⁰ x 12⁸   W.R.   BED RM.
8⁴ x 11⁰

BATH

KITCHEN
FAMILY RM.
17⁰ x 13⁶

CL.   CL.

CL.   CL.

REF'G.   DN.

CL.

GARAGE
13⁸ x 23⁴

32'-5"

BED RM.
10⁰ x 10⁰   BED RM.
10⁰ x 10⁰

LIN.
CL.

CL.

RAISED
HEARTH

LIVING RM.
18⁴ x 13⁶

WOOD FENCE   LAMP
POST

BASEMENT PLAN

Design 32198

1,193 Sq. Ft.; 23,263 Cu. Ft. - Basement
14,805 Cu. Ft. - Non-Basement

56'-0"

TERRACE

MASTER
BED RM.
10⁰ x 12⁸   W.R.   BED RM.
8⁴ x 11⁰

BATH

KITCHEN
FAMILY RM.
17⁰ x 13⁶

CL.   CL.

CL.   CL.

REF'G.   D.W.   AIR
COND

CL.

GARAGE
13⁸ x 23⁴

32'-5"

BED RM.
10⁰ x 10⁰   BED RM.
10⁰ x 10⁰

LIN.
CL.

CL.

RAISED
HEARTH

LIVING RM.
18⁴ x 13⁶

NON BASEMENT PLAN

WOOD FENCE   LAMP
POST

● Can't you just picture this delightfully proportioned traditional home sitting on your property? Surely it is an exciting thought to contemplate. And the appeal isn't just restricted to the outside, either! The floor plan is an extremely simple one. Yet it features four bedrooms, excellent storage facilities, a private wash room for the master bedroom, an in-line kitchen with a long bank of wall cupboards, a generous all-purpose family area and a raised hearth fireplace. Blueprints for this design include both basement and non-basement details for construction.

54'-0"

TERRACE

STORAGE

MASTER BED RM. 10⁰x12⁶

W.R.

BED RM. 8⁴x11⁰

KITCHEN FAMILY RM. 17⁰x13⁶

BATH

DN.

CL.

CARPORT 11⁴ x 20⁰

32'-0"

CL. CL.
CL. CL.

LIN. CL.

RAISED HEARTH

BED RM. 10⁰x10⁰

BED RM. 10⁰x10⁰

CL.

LIVING RM. 18⁴x13⁶

Design 32199

1,185 Sq. Ft.; 21,721 Cu. Ft. - Basement
13,224 Cu. Ft. - Non-Basement

BASEMENT PLAN

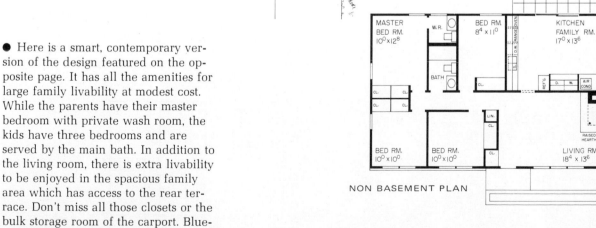

54'-0"

TERRACE

STORAGE

MASTER BED RM. 10⁰x12⁸

W.R.

BED RM. 8⁴x11⁰

KITCHEN FAMILY RM. 17⁰x13⁶

BATH

CL.

REF'G. D. W. AIR COND.

CARPORT 11⁴ x 20⁰

32'-5"

CL. CL.
CL. CL.

LIN. CL.

RAISED HEARTH

BED RM. 10⁰x10⁰

BED RM. 10⁰x10⁰

CL.

LIVING RM. 18⁴x13⁶

NON BASEMENT PLAN

● Here is a smart, contemporary version of the design featured on the opposite page. It has all the amenities for large family livability at modest cost. While the parents have their master bedroom with private wash room, the kids have three bedrooms and are served by the main bath. In addition to the living room, there is extra livability to be enjoyed in the spacious family area which has access to the rear terrace. Don't miss all those closets or the bulk storage room of the carport. Blueprints include optional basement and non-basement details.

Design 32167
864 Sq. Ft.; 16,554 Cu. Ft.

● This 36' x 24' contemporary rectangle will be economical to build whether you construct the basement design at left, 32167, or the non-basement version below, 32168.

Design 32168
864 Sq. Ft.; 9,244 Cu. Ft.

● This non-basement design features a storage room and a laundry area with cupboards above the washer and dryer. Notice the kitchen eating space.

● Here are three optional front exteriors which can be built with either the basement plan, 32160, or the non-basement plan, 32161. Whichever number you order, the blueprints will include details for all three optional front elevations. It is interesting to observe the variations in the two floor plans. Don't miss the extra storage facilities. Notice the location of the stacked washer and dryer in the non-basement plan.

Design 32160
960 Sq. Ft.; 18,394 Cu. Ft.

Design 32161
960 Sq. Ft.; 10,272 Cu. Ft.

Design 31281
1,190 Sq. Ft.; 21,920 Cu. Ft.

● Whatever you call it, contemporary or traditional, or even transitional, the prudent incorporation of newer with old design features results in a pleasant facade. The window and door detailing is obviously from an early era; while the low-pitched roof and the carport are features of relatively more recent vintage. Inside, there is an efficient plan which lends itself to the activities of the small family. As a home for a retired couple, or a young newlywed couple, this will be a fine investment. Certainly it will not require a big, expensive piece of property. The plan offers two full baths, three bedrooms, an excellent L-shaped kitchen, 23-foot living and dining area and a basement. Note side terrace.

Floor plan labels (Design 33195):

- 52'-0"
- 28'-0" / 24'-0"
- 44'-4" / 40'-0"
- BED RM. 11⁸ x 11⁸
- MASTER BED RM. 13⁰ x 11⁸
- CL.
- LIN.
- TERRACE
- BATH
- CL. / CL.
- W.R.
- BED RM. 9⁴ x 10⁰
- CL.
- REF'G
- LIN.
- KIT. 12⁰ x 8⁰
- RANGE / OVEN
- STORAGE
- DW.
- STOR. / STOR. / STOR.
- SNACK BAR
- CL.
- LIVING RM. 11⁸ x 17⁰
- FAMILY RM. 12⁰ x 11⁸
- PORCH-CARPORT 24⁰ x 24⁰
- COVERED WALK

Design 33195
1,120 Sq. Ft.; 20,440 Cu. Ft.

● This 28 x 40 foot rectangle is a fine example of how delightful and refreshing contemporary design can become. Though simple in basic construction and floor planning, this home has an abundance of exterior appeal and interior livability. Observe the low-pitched, wide overhanging roof, the attached 24 foot square covered porch/carport, the effective glass area and vertical siding, plus the raised planter. The center entrance is flanked by the formal living room and the informal, all-purpose family room. A snack bar is accessible from the kitchen. Sliding glass doors lead to the outdoor living area. In addition to the main bath there is an extra wash room handy to both the master bedroom and the kitchen.

Floor plan labels (Design 31216):

- 56'-0"
- 12'-0"
- 32'-0"
- 28'-0"
- PORCH 14⁰ x 12⁰
- TERRACE
- HOBBIES LAUND. 10⁸ x 11⁴
- W-D.
- W.R.
- RANGE / S
- DINING 11⁸ x 9⁴
- LIVING RM. 17⁰ x 15⁶
- KIT. 8⁰ x 11⁴
- REF'G
- D.W.
- BRM.
- CL. / CL.
- CL. / AIR COND.
- THRU FIREPLACE
- ENTRY HALL
- STORAGE
- COVERED WALK
- CL. / VANITY / LIN.
- BATH
- BED RM. 9⁰ x 11⁶
- BED RM. 11⁸ x 11⁶
- CARPORT 11⁸ x 24⁰

Design 31216
1,184 Sq. Ft.; 10,656 Cu. Ft.

● Whether called upon to function as a home for a retired couple or for a small family, this frame, non-basement design will provide wonderful livability. The covered walk with its adjacent planting areas makes for a pleasing approach to the front door. The thru-fireplace may be enjoyed from both formal areas—the living room and the separate dining room. Glass sliding doors lead to the cheerful enclosed porch. A pass-thru from the kitchen facilitates the serving of meals in the dining area. A wash room is conveniently located between the kitchen and hobbies/laundry room and is handy from the outdoors. The general area has an abundance of counter, cupboard and closet space.

FAMILY
DINING
9⁰ x 11⁶

KIT.
11⁰ x 8⁰

OPTIONAL BASEMENT PLAN

Design 33196
992 Sq. Ft.; 9,840 Cu. Ft.

● Here is another low-cost home which will return big dividends. Its basic rectangular shape, simple (yet attractive) overhanging roof, frame exterior and non-basement plan all add up to construction economies.

Design 32158
1,058 Sq. Ft.; 10,749 Cu. Ft.

● A fine contemporary with a low-pitched, wide overhanging roof. Note the outdoor planters, attached carport (make it a garage, if you wish) and the two storage areas.

Design 33226
1,120 Sq. Ft.; 11,760 Cu. Ft.

● Three bedrooms, 1½ baths, a laundry area, an all-purpose family room and an L-shaped kitchen with eating space are among the features of this traditional design. Back-to-back plumbing will be very economical.

Design 33227
1,164 Sq. Ft.; 13,479 Cu. Ft.

● This efficient plan contains all of the elements for a lifetime of living convenience. Of particular interest is the economical grouping of all the plumbing facilities at the rear of the plan.

Design 33208
1,152 Sq. Ft.; 21,888 Cu. Ft.

● This appealing traditional, L-shaped home has much to offer those in search of a moderately sized home which can be built within the confines of a relatively small budget. First of all, consider the charm of the exterior. Surely this will be one of the most appealing houses on the street. And little wonder. Its proportion and architectural detailing are excellent. The shutters, the window treatment, the roof lines, the planter and the fence and lamp post are all captivating features.

Design 31373
1,200 Sq. Ft.; 15,890 Cu. Ft.

● A traditional L-shaped home with an attractive recessed front entrance which leads into a floor plan where traffic patterns are most efficient. It is possible to go from one room to any other without needlessly walking through a third room. The daily household chores will be easily dispatched. The U-shaped kitchen has an abundance of cupboard and counter space, plus a pass-thru to the snack bar in the family room. The washer and dryer location is handy.

Design 31058
1,200 Sq. Ft.; 13,392 Cu. Ft.

● When you build this charming L-shaped traditionally designed home don't leave out the wood fence and lamp post. These are just the features needed to complete the picture. A porch shelters the front door which leads to the centered entry flanked by the formal living room and the informal family room. The kitchen is but a step from the separate dining room. The laundry equipment, the extra wash room and heater location are all grouped together.

Design 32570
1,176 Sq. Ft.; 26,800 Cu. Ft.

● This attractive Tudor is another economically built design which will cater admirably to the living patterns of the retired couple. In addition to the two bedrooms this plan offers a study which could double ideally as a guest room, sewing room or even serve as the TV room. The living area is a spacious L-shaped zone for formal living and dining. The efficient kitchen is handy to the front door and overlooks the front yard. It features a convenient breakfast nook for those informal meals. Handy to the entry from the garage and the yard are the stairs to the basement. Don't overlook the attractive front porch.

Design 32607
1,208 Sq. Ft.; 15,183 Cu. Ft.

● Here is an English Tudor retirement cottage. Its byword is "convenience". There are two sizable bedrooms, a full bath, plus an extra wash room. The living and dining areas are spacious and overlook both front and rear yards. Sliding glass doors in both these areas lead to the outdoor terrace. Note the fireplace in the living room. In addition to the formal dining area with its built-in china cabinet, there is a delightful breakfast eating alcove in the kitchen. The U-shaped work area is wonderfully efficient. The laundry is around the corner. Blueprints include optional basement details.

OPTIONAL BASEMENT

Design 31279
1,200 Sq. Ft.; 12,300 Cu. Ft.

● This cozy traditional ranch house is ideal for a retired couple. Its small size and one-story plan make it easy for them to enjoy and maintain. Its low cost also makes it feasible for young married couples, who, as their families and income expands, can add bedrooms to the front or side of the bedroom wing. The house provides good circulation to living, sleeping and utility zones so that no room has the interruption of cross traffic.

Design 31395
1,172 Sq. Ft.; 14,712 Cu. Ft.

● A well-zoned plan which will service the family most conveniently for many years. The front entry leads to a hall which runs all the way through the house. Note the truly fine zoning. Formal and informal livability: the living/dining room and the family room adjacent to the kitchen. Three front bedrooms serviced by a bath and a half. The washer and dryer are located in the wash room.

Design 31808
1,118 Sq. Ft.; 19,952 Cu. Ft.

● Contemporary design takes many forms. It is noted for its straight-forward simplicity and its effective use of materials. This appealing design reflects a pleasing use of brick masses and large glass areas. The low-pitched roof has a wide overhang which helps maintain that desired ground-hugging appearance. Cleverly planned, each square foot makes its contribution to complete livability. A full basement adds extra space for hobbies and recreation. The attached carport shields the service entrance and functions with the outdoor terrace.

Design 33214
1,020 Sq. Ft.; 9,530 Cu. Ft.

● This design will surely attract its full share of attention wherever built. And little wonder. It will be relatively economical to build, too. For the basic house is a 28 x 36 foot rectangle. There are sloping ceilings throughout. The carport provides bulk storage units. The family-kitchen area is unique and will be enjoyed when kitchen duties are called for or to just sit back and relax.

Design 31379
864 Sq. Ft.; 8,778 Cu. Ft.

● This low-cost, efficiently-planned, house is custom-designed for a retired person or couple. The compact arrangement of rooms all on one level makes it easy to move from one area to another, inside or out, quickly and without exertion. A large hobby and storage room is ideal for pursuing favorite projects, such as woodworking or gardening. Sliding glass doors across the back of living-dining area make terrace easily accessible from kitchen for outdoor meals and entertaining. Each of the two bedrooms has a built-in chest adjacent to closet.

Design 32156
1,064 Sq. Ft.; 20,064 Cu. Ft.

Design 31187
1,120 Sq. Ft.; 12,600 Cu. Ft.

Design 31113
1,008 Sq. Ft.; 19,737 Cu. Ft.

LEISURE LIVING HOUSES . . .

may also be referred to as vacation homes. Any presentation of one-story homes would not be complete without a chance to compare the floor planning ideas and the living style of the conventional house versus that designed for leisure living. Here is a selection of houses designed for informal living. Notice the emphasis on indoor-outdoor living relationships. Large glass areas, sloping ceilings, open planning, and dual-use space all add to the feeling of spaciousness and informality. As shown, the vacation home may be a simple rectangle, a round house, a hexagon, or an irregularly shaped structure. Your family will determine how it will use the informal living areas.

Design 32483   1,775 Sq. Ft.; 21,394 Cu. Ft.

● Floor-to-ceiling windows are a delightful attraction in the living room. They are good looking and a way to take advantage of the beautiful outdoor scenery. For more good looks, sloped ceilings, a raised hearth fireplace plus a terrace that runs the length of the house. A formal dining room is convenient to the efficient, U-shaped kitchen with a separate breakfast room. The laundry/mud room will allow immediate cleanup after a day spent fishing or on the beach. Three bedrooms! Including one with a private bath.

Design 31403 698 Sq. Ft.; 7,441 Cu. Ft.

Design 32424 1,456 Sq. Ft.; 16,760 Cu. Ft.

● Here are five outstanding second homes which, in spite of their variation in size, have many things in common. Perhaps the most significant common denominator is the location of the living area and its unrestricted view of the outdoors. Each of the designs feature a glass gable end and sloping ceiling which assures the living zone of a bright and cheerful atmosphere. A study of the sizes and the livability of these designs is interesting. They range in size from a 576 square foot, one bedroom cottage, to a 1,456 square foot lodge with four bedrooms plus two bunk rooms. Regardless of the overall size of the interior, the open planning of the living areas results in plenty of space for your family and visitors to just sit around and talk.

Design 32423 864 Sq. Ft.; 9,504 Cu. Ft.

Design 31458 576 Sq. Ft.; 5,904 Cu. Ft.

Design 31495 800 Sq. Ft.; 9,108 Cu. Ft.

173

Design 31486
480 Sq. Ft.; 4,118 Cu. Ft.

● You'll be anxious to start building this delightful little vacation home. Whether you do-it-yourself, or engage professional help, you will not have to wait long for its completion.

Design 32425
1,106 Sq. Ft.; 14,599 Cu. Ft.

● You'll adjust to living in this vacation cottage with the greatest of ease. And forevermore the by-word will be, "fun". Imagine, a thirty-one foot living room with access to a large deck!

Design 31449
1,024 Sq. Ft.; 11,264 Cu. Ft.

● If yours is a preference for a vacation home with a distinctive flair, then you need not look any further. Here is a simple and economically built 32 foot rectangle to meet your needs.

Design 31488
720 Sq. Ft.; 8,518 Cu. Ft.

● The kids won't be able to move into this vacation retreat soon enough. Two bunk rooms plus another bedroom for Mom and Dad. Open-planned living area. A real leisure-time home.

Design 31462
1,176 Sq. Ft.; 11,995 Cu. Ft.

● A second home with the informal living message readily apparent both inside and out. The zoning of this home is indeed most interesting – and practical, too. Study the plan carefully.

Design 31485
784 Sq. Ft.; 10,192 Cu. Ft.

● Here's a perfect 28 foot square that will open up new dimensions in living for its occupants. A fine, lower budget version of 31449 on the opposing page yet retaining many of the fine qualities.

Design 32439
1,312 Sq. Ft.; 17,674 Cu. Ft.

● A wonderfully organized plan with an exterior that will command the attention of each and every passerby. And what will catch the eye? Certainly the roof lines and the pointed glass gable end wall will be noticed immediately. The delightful deck will be quickly noticed, too. Inside a visitor will be thrilled by the spaciousness of the huge living room. The ceilings slope upward to the exposed ridge beam. A free-standing fireplace will make its contribution to a cheerful atmosphere. What could improve upon the sleeping zone when it has two bedrooms, two bunk rooms, two full baths, two built-in chests and fine closet space?

Design 32417
1,520 Sq. Ft.; 19,952 Cu. Ft.

● Have you ever seen a vacation home design that is anything quite like this one? Probably not! The picturesque exterior is dominated by a projecting gable with its wide, overhanging roof acting as a dramatic sun visor for the large glass area below. Effectively balancing this 20 foot center section are two 20 foot wings. Inside, and below the high, sloping, beamed ceiling is the huge living area. In addition to the living--dining area, there is the spacious sunken lounge. This pleasant area has a built-in seating arrangement and a cozy fireplace. The parents' and children's sleeping areas are separated and each has a full bath.

Design 32418
1,424 Sq. Ft.; 17,891 Cu. Ft.

● You'll search a long time before locating a vacation home that is any more exciting than this fascinating angular retreat. Whatever its setting, it will command attention and also provide its happy owners with a lifetime of carefree living. The soaring roof lines, the cedar shakes, the appealing glass areas and the sloping, beamed ceilings are features. Three bedrooms and a centered bath are clustered together. Family activities will take place in the spacious living room.

Design 32479
1,547 Sq. Ft.; 14,878 Cu. Ft.

● Here is a unique round house with an equally unique floor plan. The centrally located family room is the focal point. There is much to study and admire in this plan. For instance, the use of space is most efficient. Notice the strategic location of the kitchen. Don't miss the storage room and laundry. Observe the snack bar, the two-way fireplace, the separate dining room and the two full baths. Fixed glass windows at the beamed ceiling provide natural light from above for the family room.

Design 32457
1,288 Sq. Ft.; 13,730 Cu. Ft.

● Leisure living will be graciously experienced in this second home. The wide overhanging roof affords protection from the sun. This home is a perfect square measuring 36 x 36 feet, not counting the clipped corner. The 23 foot square living room enjoys a great view of the surrounding environment by virtue of the expanses of glass. "Open planning" adds to the spaciousness of the interior. Three bedrooms are served by two full baths which are accessible to other areas. The kitchen, looking out upon the water, will be a delight. What great planning for a leisure-time second home.

Design 32461
1,400 Sq. Ft.; 13,742 Cu. Ft.

● If you have the urge to make your vacation home one that has a distinctive flair of individuality, you should give consideration to this design. Not only will you love the unique exterior appeal of your new home but, also, the exceptional living patterns offered by the interior. Here, the basic living area is a hexagon. The sleeping wings with bath are added to this space conscious geometric shape.

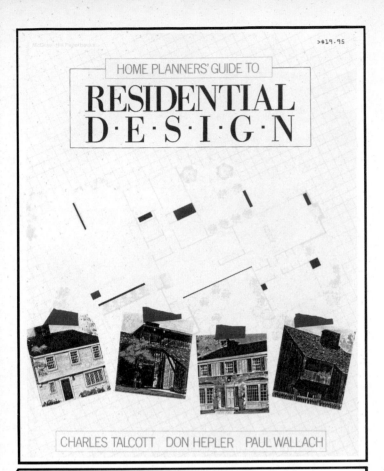

HOME PLANNERS' GUIDE TO

RESIDENTIAL D·E·S·I·G·N

CHARLES TALCOTT   DON HEPLER   PAUL WALLACH

Announcing-

A "MUST" Book for Anyone Involved in the Planning of a New Home

This book features a wealth of information vital to the successful planning of a new home. Discussed in a highly illustrated manner, is a great variety of subjects concerning residential design and planning. Written and edited specifically for use during the early planning and pre-construction stages of the building program, this book may save you many times its cost. In addition to giving a layman's overview of the architectural side of residential design, it helps the reader give due consideration to the innumerable budgetary and livability aspects of the planning process. A CHECKLIST FOR PLAN SELECTION lists over 650 items that will guide and help assure proper decision-making which involve the myriad of subjects influencing proper residential design and planning.
224 pages, soft cover.

A Most Rewarding and Money-Saving Book.   **$21.95** Postpaid

Contents

Design 31497
1,292 Sq. Ft.; 13,730 Cu. Ft.

● This attractive vacation home will serve your family ideally for many years. The segregated sleeping area will provide a lot of privacy from the family activities. Notice the master bedroom with a full bath and a walk-in closet. Two other bedrooms and a full bathroom also will be found. Through the entry hall, you come to the large living room with fireplace. Nearby is the dining area and kitchen. A few steps away is a washroom. Notice that this whole area is accented by a sloped ceiling as in the master bedroom. Also take note of the storage area.

Design 31479
1,360 Sq. Ft.; 17,026 Cu. Ft.

● This attractive vacation home will serve your family ideally for many years. The segregated sleeping area will provide a lot of privacy from the family activities. Notice the master bedroom with a full bath and walk-in closet. Two other bedrooms and a full bathroom also will be found. Through the entry hall, you come to the large living room with fireplace. Nearby is the dining area and kitchen. A few steps away is a washroom. Notice that this whole area is accented by a sloped ceiling as in the master bedroom. Also take note of the storage area.

180

All The "TOOLS" You And Your Builder Need. . .

1. THE PLAN BOOKS

Home Planners' unique Design Category Series makes it easy to look at and study only the types of designs for which you and your family have an interest. Each of six plan books features a specific type of home, namely: Two-Story, 1½ Story, One-Story Over 2000 Sq. Ft., One-Story Under 2000 Sq. Ft., Multi-Levels and Vacation Homes. In addition to the convenient Design Category Series, there is an impressive selection of other current titles. While the home plans featured in these books are also to be found in the Design Category Series, they, too, are edited for those with special tastes and requirements. Your family will spend many enjoyable hours reviewing the delightfully designed exteriors and the practical floor plans. Surely your home or office library should include a selection of these popular plan books. Your complete satisfaction is guaranteed.

2. THE CONSTRUCTION BLUEPRINTS

There are blueprints available for each of the designs published in Home Planners' current plan books. Depending upon the size, the style and the type of home, each set of blueprints consists of from five to ten large sheets. Only by studying the blueprints is it possible to give complete and final consideration to the proper selection of a design for your next home. The blueprints provide the opportunity for all family members to familiarize themselves with the features of all exterior elevations, interior elevations and details, all dimensions, special built-in features and effects. They also provide a full understanding of the materials to be used and/or selected. The low-cost of our blueprints makes it possible and indeed, practical, to study in detail a number of different sets of blueprints before deciding upon which design to build.

3. THE MATERIALS LIST

A list of materials is an integral part of the plan package. It comprises the last sheet of each set of blueprints and serves as a handy reference during the period of construction. Of course, at the pricing and the material ordering stages, it is indispensable.

4. THE SPECIFICATION OUTLINE

Each order for blueprints is accompanied by one Specification Outline. You and your builder will find this a time-saving tool when deciding upon your own individual specifications. An important reference document should you wish to write your own specifications.

5. THE PLUMBING & ELECTRICAL PACKAGE

The construction blueprints you order from Home Planners, Inc. include locations for all plumbing fixtures — sinks, lavatories, tubs, showers, water closets, laundry trays, hot water heaters, etc. The blueprints also show the locations of all electrical switches, plugs, and outlets. These plumbing and electrical details are sufficient to present to your local contractor for discussions about your individual specifications and subsequent installations in conformance with local codes. However, for those who wish to acquaint themselves with many of the intricacies of residential plumbing and electrical details and installations, Home Planners, Inc. has made available this package. We do not recommend that the layman attempt to do his own plumbing and electrical work. It is, nevertheless, advisable that owners be as knowledgeable as possible about each of these disciplines. The entire family will appreciate the educational value of these low-cost, easy-to-understand details.

The Design Category Series

360 TWO STORY HOMES

English Tudors, Early American Salt Boxes, Gambrels, Farmhouses, Southern Colonials, Georgians, French Mansards, Contemporaries. Interesting floor plans for both small and large families. Efficient kitchens, 2 to 6 bedrooms, family rooms, libraries, extra baths, mud rooms. Homes for all budgets.

1.

288 Pages, $6.95

150 1½ STORY HOMES

Cape Cod, Williamsburg, Georgian, Tudor and Contemporary versions. Low budget and country-estate feature sections. Expandable family plans. Formal and informal living and dining areas along with gathering rooms. Spacious, country kitchens. Indoor-outdoor livability with covered porches and functional terraces.

2.

128 Pages, $3.95

210 ONE STORY HOMES OVER 2,000 Sq. Ft.

All popular styles. Including Spanish, Western, Tudor, French, and other traditional versions. Contemporaries. Gracious, family living patterns. Sunken living rooms, master bedroom suites, atriums, courtyards, pools. Fine indoor-outdoor living relationships. For modest country-estate budgets.

3.

192 Pages, $4.95

315 ONE STORY HOMES UNDER 2,000 Sq. Ft.

A great selection of traditional and contemporary exteriors for medium and restricted budgets. Efficient, practical floor plans. Gathering rooms, formal and informal living and dining rooms, mud rooms, indoor-outdoor livability. Economically built homes. Designs with bonus space livability for growing families.

4.

192 Pages, $4.95

215 MULTI-LEVEL HOMES

For new dimensions in family living. A captivating variety of exterior styles, exciting floor plans for flat and sloping sites. Exposed lower levels. Balconies, decks. Plans for the active family. Upper level lounges, excellent bath facilities. Sloping ceilings. Functional outdoor terraces. For all building budgets.

5.

192 Pages, $4.95

223 VACATION HOMES

Features A-Frames, Chalets, Hexagons, economical rectangles. One and two stories plus multi-levels. Lodges for year 'round livability. From 480 to 3238 sq. ft. Cottages sleeping to 22. For flat or sloping sites. Spacious, open planning. Over 600 illustrations. 120 Pages in full color. Cluster home selection. For lakeshore or woodland leisure living.

6.

176 Pages, $4.95

The Exterior Style Series

330 EARLY AMERICAN PLANS

Our new *Essential Guide to Early American Home Plans* traces Early American architecture from our Colonial Past to Traditional styles popular today with a written history of designs and colorful sections devoted to styles. Many of our designs are patterned after historic homes.

7.

304 Pages, $9.95

335 CONTEMPORARY HOME PLANS

Our new *Essential Guide to Contemporary Home Plans* offers a colorful directory to modern architecture, including a history of American Contemporary styling and more than 335 home plans of all sizes and popular designs. 304 colorful pages! Must reading for contemporary lifestyles.

8.

304 Pages, $9.95

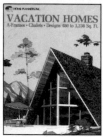

135 ENGLISH TUDOR HOMES

and other Popular Family Plans is a favorite of many. The current popularity of the English Tudor home design is phenomenal. Here is a book which is loaded with Tudors for all budgets. There are one-story, 1½ and two-story designs, plus multi-levels and hillsides from 1,176–3,849 sq. ft.

9.

104 Pages, $3.95

The Budget Series

175 LOW BUDGET HOMES

A special selection of home designs for the modest or restricted building budget. An excellent variety of Traditional and Contemporary designs. One-story, 1½ and two-story and split-level homes. Three, four and five bedrooms. Family rooms, extra baths, formal and informal dining rooms. Basement and non-basement designs. Attached garages and covered porches.

11.

96 Pages, $2.95

165 AFFORDABLE HOME PLANS

This outstanding book was specially edited with a wide selection of houses and plans for those with a medium building budget. While none of these designs are considered low-cost; neither do they require an unlimited budget to build. Square footages range from 1,428. Exteriors of Tudor, French, Early American, Spanish and Contemporary are included.

12.

112 Pages, $2.95

142 HOME DESIGNS FOR EXPANDED BUILDING BUDGETS

A family's ability to finance and need for a larger home grows as its size and income increases. This selection highlights designs which house an average square footage of 2,551. One-story plans average 2,069; two-stories, 2,738; multi-levels, 2,825. Spacious homes featuring raised hearth fireplaces, open planning and efficient kitchens.

13.

112 Pages, $2.95

General Interest Titles

ENCYCLOPEDIA - 450 PLANS

For those who wish to review and study perhaps the largest selection of designs available in a single volume. Varying exterior styles, plus interesting and practical floor plans for all building budgets. Formal, informal living patterns; indoor-outdoor livability; small, growing and large family facilities.

15.

320 Pages, $9.95

244 HOUSE PLANS FOR BETTER LIVING

Special 40th Anniversary Edition with over 650 illustrations. Sectionalized to highlight special interest groups of designs. A fine introduction to our special interest titles. All styles, sizes, and types of homes are represented. Designs feature gathering rooms, country kitchens, second-floor lounges.

16.

192 Pages $3.50

255 HOME DESIGNS FOR FAMILY LIVING

In addition to the plans that cater to a variety of family living patterns and budgets, there are special sections on vacation homes, earth-sheltered homes, sun-oriented living, and shared livability. One, 1½; two-story, and multi-level designs. The book includes over 700 illustrations.

17.

192 Pages, $3.50

COLOR PORTFOLIO - 310 DESIGNS

An expanded full-color guide to our most popular Early American, Spanish, French, Tudor, Contemporary, and modern Trend home designs. 310 home plans of all popular styles and sizes. Includes energy-efficient designs. Plans for varying building budgets. One, 1½, two-story, and split-level designs for all terrain. This is our largest full-color book with our newest trend-setting designs and other favorites. It's must reading for the serious home planner.

18.

288 Pages in Full Color, $12.95

136 SPANISH & WESTERN HOME DESIGNS

Stucco exteriors, arches, tile roofs, wide-overhangs, courtyards and rambling ranches are characteristics which make this design selection distinctive. These sun-country designs highlight indoor-outdoor relationships. Solar oriented livability is featured.

10.

120 Pages, $3.95

PLAN BOOKS are a valuable tool for anyone who plans to build a new home. After you have selected a home design that satisfies your list of requirements, you can order blueprints for further study.

115 HOME DESIGNS FOR UNLIMITED BUILDING BUDGETS

This book will appeal to those with large families and the desire and wherewithal to satisfy all the family needs, plus most of their wants. The upscale designs in this portfolio average 3,132 square feet. One-story designs average 2,796 sq. ft.; 1½-story, 3,188 sq. ft.; two-story, 3,477 sq. ft.; multi-level, 3,532 sq. ft. Truly designs for elegant living.

14.

112 Pages, $2.95

HOME PLANNERS, INC.

Dept. BK, 23761 Research Drive
Farmington Hills, Michigan 48024

Please mail me the following:

THE DESIGN CATEGORY SERIES - A great series of books specially edited by design type and size. Each book features interesting sections to further enhance the study of design styles, sizes and house types. A fine addition to the home or office library. Complete collection - over 1250 designs.

1. _____ 360 Two Story Homes @ $6.95 ea. . . . . $_____
2. _____ 150 1½ Story Homes @ $3.95 ea. . . . . $_____
3. _____ 210 One Story Homes - Over 2,000 Sq. Ft. @ $4.95 ea. . . $_____
4. _____ 315 One Story Homes - Under 2,000 Sq. Ft. @ $4.95 ea. . $_____
5. _____ 215 Multi-Level Homes @ $4.95 ea. . . . . $_____
6. _____ 223 Vacation Homes @ $4.95 ea. . . . . $_____

OTHER CURRENT TITLES - The interesting series of plan books listed below have been edited to appeal to various style preferences and budget considerations. The majority of the designs highlighted in these books also may be found in the Design Category Series.

The Exterior Style Series-
7. _____ 330 Early American Home Plans @ $9.95 ea. . . . . $_____
8. _____ 335 Contemporary Home Plans @ $9.95 ea. . . . . $_____
9. _____ 135 English Tudor Homes @ $3.95 ea. . . . . $_____
10. _____ 136 Spanish & Western Home Designs @ $3.95 ea. . . . . $_____

The Budget Series-
11. _____ 175 Low Budget Homes @ $2.95 ea. . . . . $_____
12. _____ 165 Affordable Home Plans @ $2.95 ea. . . . . $_____
13. _____ 142 Home Designs for Expanded Budgets @ $2.95 ea. . $_____
14. _____ 115 Home Designs for Unlimited Budgets @ $2.95 ea. . $_____

General Interest Titles-
15. _____ Encyclopedia of Home Designs - 450 Designs @ $9.95 ea. $_____
16. _____ 244 House Plans for Better Living @ $3.50 ea. . . . . $_____
17. _____ 255 Home Designs for Family Living @ $3.50 ea. . . . . . $_____

Full Color Book-
18. _____ Color Portfolio of Houses & Plans - 310 Designs @ $12.95 ea. $_____

Sub Total $_____

Michigan Residents kindly add 4% sales tax $_____

Add for postage and handling $___1.00___

TOTAL—Check enclosed $_____

Your order will be processed and shipped within 48 hours

MAIL TODAY

SATISFACTION GUARANTEED!

Please Print

Name _____

Address _____

City _____ State _____ Zip _____

In Canada Mail To: Home Planners, Inc., 20 Cedar St. North, Kitchener, Ontario N2H 2W8

CV3BK

Frontal Sheet

Foundation Plans

Detailed Floor Plans

House Cross-Sections

Interior Elevations

Exterior Elevations

Material List

The Blueprints

1. FRONTAL SHEET.
Artist's landscaped sketch of the exterior and ink-line floor plans are on the frontal sheet of each set of blueprints.

2. FOUNDATION PLAN.
¼" Scale basement and foundation plan. All necessary notations and dimensions. Plot plan diagram for locating house on building site.

3. DETAILED FLOOR PLAN.
¼" Scale first and second floor plans with complete dimensions. Cross-section detail keys. Diagrammatic layout of electrical outlets and switches.

4. HOUSE CROSS-SECTIONS.
Large scale sections of foundation, interior and exterior walls, floors and roof details for design and construction control.

5. INTERIOR ELEVATIONS.
Large scale interior details of the complete kitchen cabinet design, bathrooms, powder room, laundry, fireplaces, paneling, beam ceilings, built-in cabinets, etc.

6. EXTERIOR ELEVATIONS.
¼" Scale exterior elevation drawings of front, rear, and both sides of the house. All exterior materials and details are shown to indicate the complete design and proportions of the house.

7. MATERIAL LIST.
Complete lists of all materials required for the construction of the house as designed are included in each set of blueprints.

THIS BLUEPRINT PACKAGE
will help you and your family take a major step forward in the final appraisal and planning of your new home. Only by spending many enjoyable and informative hours studying the numerous details included in the complete package, will you feel sure of, and comfortable with, your commitment to build your new home. To assure successful and productive consultation with your builder and/or architect, reference to the various elements of the blueprint package is a must. The blueprints, material list and specification outline will save much consultation time and expense. Don't be without them.

The Material List

With each set of blueprints you order you will receive a material list. Each list shows you the quantity, type and size of the non-mechanical materials required to build your home. It also tells you where these materials are used. This makes the blueprints easy to understand.

Influencing the mechanical requirements are geographical differences in availability of materials, local codes, methods of installation and individual preferences. Because of these factors, your local heating, plumbing and electrical contractors can supply you with necessary material take-offs for their particular trades.

Material lists simplify your material ordering and enable you to get quicker price quotations from your builder and material dealer. Because the material list is an integral part of each set of blueprints, it is not available separately.

Among the materials listed:

• Masonry, Veneer & Fireplace • Framing Lumber • Roofing & Sheet Metal • Windows & Door Frames • Exterior Trim & Insulation • Tile Work, Finish Floors • Interior Trim, Kitchen Cabinets • Rough & Finish Hardware

The Specification Outline

This fill-in type specification lists over 150 phases of home construction from excavating to painting and includes wiring, plumbing, heating and air-conditioning. It consists of 16 pages and will prove invaluable for specifying to your builder the exact materials, equipment and methods of construction you want in your new home. One Specification Outline is included free with each order for blueprints. Additional Specification Outlines are available at $3.00 each.

CONTENTS
• General Instructions, Suggestions and Information • Excavating and Grading • Masonry and Concrete Work • Sheet Metal Work • Carpentry, Millwork, Roofing, and Miscellaneous Items • Lath and Plaster or Drywall Wallboard • Schedule for Room Finishes • Painting and Finishing • Tile Work • Electrical Work • Plumbing • Heating and Air-Conditioning

The Plumbing & Electrical Package

Consists of Large 24" x 36" Sheets for Easy Reference.
Color-Coded for Quick Recognition
of Details.

For those who wish to acquaint themselves
with many of the intricacies of
residential plumbing and electrical
details and installations.
An invaluable tool and
great supplement to
the blueprint
package.

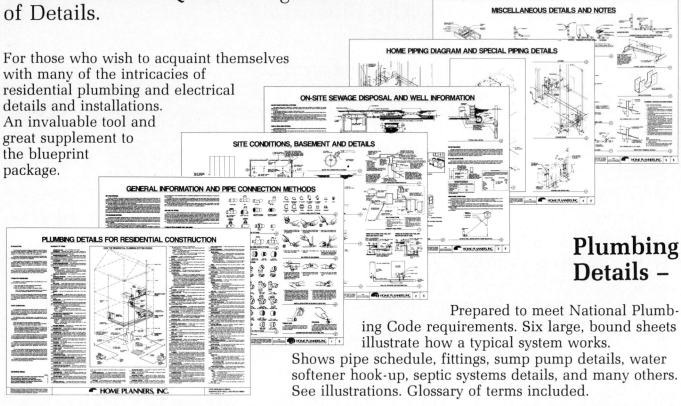

Plumbing Details –

Prepared to meet National Plumbing Code requirements. Six large, bound sheets illustrate how a typical system works.
Shows pipe schedule, fittings, sump pump details, water softener hook-up, septic systems details, and many others. See illustrations. Glossary of terms included.

Only $12.95

Of Great Educational Value to the
Entire Family.
Order Both Sets

only
$19.95
(Save $5.95)

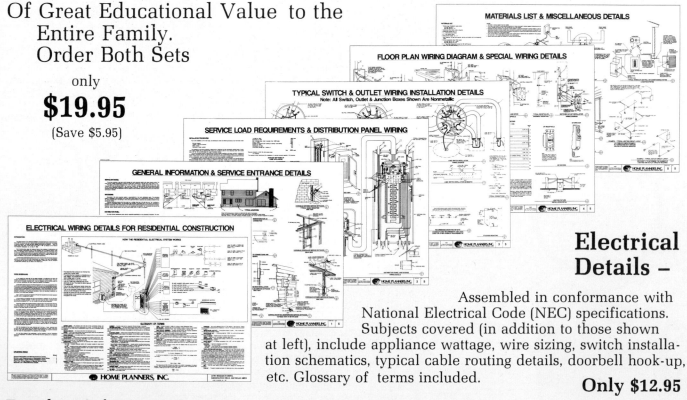

Electrical Details –

Assembled in conformance with National Electrical Code (NEC) specifications. Subjects covered (in addition to those shown at left), include appliance wattage, wire sizing, switch installation schematics, typical cable routing details, doorbell hook-up, etc. Glossary of terms included.

Only $12.95

To order, see form on next page.

Before You Order

1. STUDY THE DESIGNS . . . found in Home Planners books. As you review these delightful custom homes, you should keep in mind the total living requirements of your family — both indoors and outdoors. Although we do not make changes in plans, many minor changes can be made prior to the period of construction. If major changes are involved to satisfy your personal requirements, you should consider ordering one set of blueprints and having them redrawn locally. Consultation with your architect is strongly advised when contemplating major changes.

2. HOW TO ORDER BLUEPRINTS . . . After you have chosen the design that satisfies your requirements, or if you have selected one that you wish to study in more detail, simply clip the accompanying order blank and mail with your remittance. However, if it is not convenient for you to send a check or money order, you can use your credit card, or merely indicate C.O.D. shipment. Postman will collect all charges, including postage

and C.O.D. fee C.O.D. shipments are not permitted to Canada or foreign countries. Should time be of essence, as it sometimes is with many of our customers, your telephone order usually can be processed and shipped in the next day's mail. Simply call toll free 1-800-521-6797, (Michigan residents call collect 0-313-477-1850).

3. OUR SERVICE . . . Home Planners makes every effort to process and ship each order for blueprints and books within 48 hours. Because of this, we have deemed it unnecessary to acknowledge receipt of our customers orders. See order coupon for the postage and handling charges for surface mail, air mail or foreign mail.

4. A NOTE REGARDING REVERSE BLUEPRINTS . . . As a special service to those

wishing to build in reverse of the plan as shown, we do include an extra set of reversed blueprints for only $30.00 additional with each order. Even though the lettering and dimensions appear backward on reversed blueprints, they make a handy reference because they show the house just as it's being built in reverse from the standard blueprints — thereby helping you visualize the home better.

5. OUR EXCHANGE POLICY . . . Since blueprints are printed up in specific response to your individual order, we cannot honor requests for refunds. However, the first set of blueprints in any order (or the one set in a single set order) for a given design may be exchanged for a set of another design at a fee of $20.00 plus $3.00 for postage and handling via surface mail; $4.00 via air mail.

How many sets of blueprints should be ordered?

This question is often asked. The answer can range anywhere from 1 to 8 sets, depending upon circumstances. For instance, a single set of blueprints of your favorite design is sufficient to study the house in greater detail. On the other hand, if you are planning to get cost estimates, or if you are planning to build, you may need as many as eight sets of blueprints. Because the first set of blueprints in each order is $125.00, and because additional sets of the same design in each order are only $30.00 each (and with package sets even more economical), you save considerably by ordering your total requirements now. To help you determine the exact number of sets, please refer to the handy check list.

How Many Blueprints Do You Need?

___**OWNER'S SET(S)**

___**BUILDER** (Usually requires at least 3 sets: 1 as legal document; 1 for inspection; and at least 1 for tradesmen — usually more.)

___**BUILDING PERMIT** (Sometimes 2 sets are required.)

___**MORTGAGE SOURCE** (Usually 1 set for a conventional mortgage; 3 sets for F.H.A. or V.A. type mortgages.)

___**SUBDIVISION COMMITTEE** (If any.)

___**TOTAL NO. SETS REQUIRED**

Blueprint Ordering Hotline –

Phone toll free: 1-800-521-6797.
Orders received by 11 a.m. (Detroit time) will be processed the same day and shipped to you the following day. Use of this line restricted to blueprint ordering only. Michigan residents simply call collect 0-313-477-1850.

Kindly Note: When ordering by phone, please state Order Form Key No. located in box at lower left corner of blueprint order form.

In Canada Mail To:
Home Planners, Inc., 20 Cedar St. North Kitchener, Ontario N2H 2W8
Phone: (519) 743-4169

TO: **HOME PLANNERS, INC., 23761 RESEARCH DRIVE FARMINGTON HILLS, MICHIGAN 48024**

Please rush me the following:

_____ SET(S) BLUEPRINTS FOR DESIGN NO(S). _____ $_____
Single Set, $125.00; Additional Identical Sets in Same Order $30.00 ea.
4 Set Package of Same Design, $175.00 (Save $40.00) 8 Set Package of Same Design, $225.00 (Save ($110.00) Material Lists & Specification Outline included.

_____ SPECIFICATION OUTLINES @ $3.00 EACH . . . . $_____

_____ DETAIL SETS @ $12.95 ea. or both @ $19.95: ☐ PLUMBING ☐ELECTRICAL $_____

Michigan Residents add 4% sales tax $_____

FOR POSTAGE AND HANDLING PLEASE CHECK ✓ & REMIT
☐ $3.00 Added to Order for Surface Mail (UPS) – Any Mdse.
☐ $4.00 Added for Priority Mail of One-Three Sets of Blueprints.
☐ $6.00 Added for Priority Mail of Four or more Sets of Blueprints.
☐ For Canadian orders add $2.00 to above applicable rates.
$_____

☐ C.O.D. PAY POSTMAN
(C.O.D. Within U.S.A. Only)   TOTAL in U.S.A. funds $_____

PLEASE PRINT
Name _____
Street _____
City _____ State _____ Zip _____

CREDIT CARD ORDERS ONLY: Fill in the boxes below   Prices subject to change without notice

Credit Card No. ☐☐☐☐☐☐☐☐☐☐☐☐☐☐☐☐☐☐ Expiration Date Month/Year ☐☐☐☐

CHECK ONE: ☐ *VISA* ☐ MasterCard
Order Form Key CV3BP _____
Your Signature

BLUEPRINT ORDERS SHIPPED WITHIN 48 HOURS OF RECEIPT!

TO: **HOME PLANNERS, INC., 23761 RESEARCH DRIVE FARMINGTON HILLS, MICHIGAN 48024**

Please rush me the following:

_____ SET(S) BLUEPRINTS FOR DESIGN NO(S). _____ $_____
Single Set, $125.00; Additional Identical Sets in Same Order $30.00 ea.
4 Set Package of Same Design, $175.00 (Save $40.00) 8 Set Package of Same Design, $225.00 (Save $110.00) Material Lists & Specification Outline included.

_____ SPECIFICATION OUTLINES @ $3.00 EACH . . . . $_____

_____ DETAIL SETS @ $12.95 ea. or both @ $19.95: ☐ PLUMBING ☐ELECTRICAL $_____

Michigan Residents add 4% sales tax $_____

FOR POSTAGE AND HANDLING PLEASE CHECK ✓ & REMIT
☐ $3.00 Added to Order for Surface Mail (UPS) – Any Mdse.
☐ $4.00 Added for Priority Mail of One-Three Sets of Blueprints.
☐ $6.00 Added for Priority Mail of Four or more Sets of Blueprints.
☐ For Canadian orders add $2.00 to above applicable rates.
$_____

☐ C.O.D. PAY POSTMAN
(C.O.D. Within U.S.A. Only)   TOTAL in U.S.A. funds $_____

PLEASE PRINT
Name _____
Street _____
City _____ State _____ Zip _____

CREDIT CARD ORDERS ONLY: Fill in the boxes below   Prices subject to change without notice

Credit Card No. ☐☐☐☐☐☐☐☐☐☐☐☐☐☐☐☐☐☐ Expiration Date Month/Year ☐☐☐☐

CHECK ONE: ☐ *VISA* ☐ MasterCard
Order Form Key CV3BP _____
Your Signature

BONUS LIVABILITY . . .

for future expansion can result by allowing for the development of a second level of livability. Each of the following designs delivers complete one-story living and gives the appearance of being a one-story house. However, with the development of what would be unused attic space, additional sleeping facilities can be gained. These houses can be of minimal, or expanded, square footage on the first floor. Later as family size grows, or financial constraints lessen, the total livability can be considerably increased. Note the examples of how bonus space may be developed on a lower level. The basements of many one-story homes can be exposed to provide this bonus livability.

Design 32563
1,500 Sq. Ft. - First Floor
690 Sq. Ft. - Second Floor
38,243 Cu. Ft.

● This charming Cape Cod definately will capture your heart with its warm appeal. This home offers you and your family a lot of livability. Upon entering this home, to your left, is a nice-sized living room with fireplace. Adjacent is a dining room. An efficient kitchen and a large, farm kitchen eating area with fireplace will be enjoyed by all. A unique feature on this floor is the master bedroom with a full bath and walk-in closet. Also take notice of the first floor laundry, the pantry and a study for all of your favorite books. Note the sliding glass doors in the farm kitchen and master bedroom. Upstairs you'll find two bedrooms, one with a walk-in closet. Also here, a sitting room and a full bath are available. Lastly, this design accommodates a three car garage.

Design 32761 1,242 Sq. Ft. - Main Level
1,242 Sq. Ft. - Lower Level; 25,045 Cu. Ft.

● Here is another one-story that doubles its livability by exposing the lowest level at the rear. Formal living is on the main level and informal living, the activity room and study, on the lower level. Observe the wonderful outdoor living facilities. The deck acts as a cover for the terrace.

TERRACE

ACTIVITIES RM. 14⁰ x 17⁶

STUDY 15¹⁰ x 10⁰

CL.

STORAGE

UP

BED RM. 10¹⁰ x 13¹⁰

BED RM. 11² x 12⁸

LINEN

BATH

MECH. RM.

AIR COND.

WALK IN CLOSET

CL.

VANITY

CL.

UNEX.

UNEX.

50'-0"

DECK

LIVING RM. 14⁴ x 17⁶

DINING RM. 10⁰ x 10⁰

NOOK 8⁸ x 10⁰

BALCONY

RAILING

KITCHEN 12⁰ x 13⁰

MASTER BED RM. 11⁸ x 15⁰

DN

REF.

BCL. OVEN RANGE

BATH

CL.

LIN.

CL.

ENTRY

WASH RM.

SERVICE ENTRANCE

LT. WASH DRY

LAUNDRY

CL.

PORCH

CURB

STORAGE

GARAGE 21⁴ x 21⁸

52'-0"

Design 31372
768 Sq. Ft. - First Floor
432 Sq. Ft. - Second Floor
17,280 Cu. Ft.

● Low cost livability could hardly ask for more. Here is an enchanting Colonial exterior and a four bedroom floor plan. Note stairs to basement and carport.

CARPORT 12⁰ x 20⁰

FAMILY KITCHEN 13⁰ x 11⁶

BATH

BED RM. 10⁰ x 11⁶

BRM. RANGE
REF'G

LIVING RM. 16⁰ x 11⁶

BED RM. 11⁸ x 9⁰

12'-0"   32'-0"   29'-0"   24'-0"

BATH   LIN.

BED RM. 13⁰ x 11⁴

DN.

BED RM. 10⁴ x 11⁴

DRESS. ALCOVE 4⁸ x 5⁸

DRESS. ALCOVE 9⁴ x 5⁸

CL.   CL.   CL.

BATH   LIN.

TOYS

BED RM. 12⁴ x 12⁰

DN.   CL.   CL.

BED RM. 14⁸ x 12⁰

CHEST   CHEST

36'-0"   22'-0"

TERRACE

GARAGE 21⁸ x 19⁴

BED RM. 10⁰ x 11⁶

CL.

KITCHEN - DINING 17⁰ x 11⁶

RANGE
REF'G

BATH
BRM.

24'-5"

BED RM. 12⁴ x 11⁶

LIN.   CL.   DN.   CL.   UP

LIVING RM. 17⁰ x 11⁶

TOYS   P.

Design 33189 884 Sq. Ft. - First Floor
598 Sq. Ft. - Second Floor; 18,746 Cu. Ft.

● Four bedrooms, two baths, a large kitchen/dining area, plenty of closets, a full basement and an attached two-car garage are among the highlights of this design. Note the uniqueness of the second floor.

Design 31394

832 Sq. Ft. - First Floor
512 Sq. Ft. - Second Floor
19,385 Cu. Ft.

● The growing family with a restricted building budget will find this a great investment - a convenient living floor plan inside an attractively designed facade.

Design 32510

1,191 Sq. Ft. - First Floor
533 Sq. Ft. - Second Floor
27,500 Cu. Ft.

● The pleasant in-line kitchen is flanked by a separate dining room and a family room. The master bedroom is on the first floor with two more bedrooms upstairs.

Design 32718
1,941 Sq. Ft. - First Floor
791 Sq. Ft. - Second Floor
49,895 Cu. Ft.

● You and your family will love the new living patterns you'll experience in this story-and-a-half. The master bedroom has a compartmented bath with both tub and stall shower. There is a unique, sunken conversation pit. This cozy area has a planter, built-in seat and a view of the thru-fireplace, opening to the gathering room as well. Here, the ceiling slopes to the second floor lounge which looks down into the gathering room.

● This cozy Tudor adaptation is inviting. Its friendly demeanor seems to say, "welcome". Upon admittance to the front entrance hall, even the most casual of visitors will be filled with anticipation at the prospect of touring the house. A great feature is the location of the living, dining, kitchen and family rooms across the back of the house.

Design 32278
1,804 Sq. Ft. - First Floor
939 Sq. Ft. - Second Floor; 44,274 Cu. Ft.